T0235892

INTERNATIONAL CENTRE FOR MECHANICAL SCIENCES

COURSES AND LECTURES - No. 188

N. J. A. SLOANE

BELL LABORATORIES, NEW JERSEY

A SHORT COURSE ON ERROR CORRECTING CODES

UDINE 1975

SPRINGER-VERLAG WIEN GMBH

This work is subject to copyright.

All rights are reserved,

whether the whole or part of the material is concerned

specifically those of translation, reprinting, re-use of illustrations,

broadcasting, reproduction by photocopying machine

or similar means, and storage in data banks.

© 1975 by Springer-Verlag Wien

Originally published by Springer - Verlag   Wien - New York in 1975

ISBN 978-3-211-81303-4   ISBN 978-3-7091-2864-0 (eBook)
DOI 10.1007/978-3-7091-2864-0

PREFACE

The following lectures were given in July 1973 at the Summer School on Data Transmission at the "International Centre for Mechanical Sciences", Udine, Italy. The author would like to express his appreciation to Professor Giuseppe Longo, who organized this set of courses, and to Professor Luigi Sobrero, the Secretary General of the Centre, for their hospitality and for making this work possible.

N.J.A. Sloane

§§ 1 INTRODUCTION

The Coding Problem and Its History

§ 1.1 Definition and Examples

(1.1.1) **Definition** An (n,M,d) **code** is a set of M binary vectors of length n, called **codewords**, such that any two codewords differ in at least d places. n is called the (**block**) **length** of the code, and d is the **minimum distance** of the code. R = $\log_2$ M/n is called the **rate** of the code, for reasons we shall see in §§2.

Examples

00000, 11111 is a (5,2,5) code. (The same symbol is repeated 5 times - this is a repetition code). (1.1.2)

```
000
011    is a (3,4,2) code.
101
110
```
(1.1.3)

```
0000000
1110100
0111010
0011101
1001110         (1.1.4)
0100111
1010011
1101001

is a (7,8,4) code
```

```
0000000
1110100
0111010
0011101
1001110
0100111
1010011
1101001
0001011         (1.1.5)
1000101
1100010
0110001
1011000
0101100
0010110
1111111

is a (7,16,3) Hamming code
(see §5.8).
```

	00000000	11111111
	11000000	00111111
	10100000	01011111
(1.1.6)	10010000	01101111
	10001000	01110111
	10000100	01111011
	10000010	01111101
	10000001	01111110

is an (8,16,2) bad (but interesting!) code (see § 2.3).

(1.1.7) Hadamard Codes

A **Hadamard matrix** H_n is an n x n matrix with entries +1, -1 such that $H_n H_n^T = nI$. (I denotes a unit matrix, and H_n^T is the transpose of H_n.) Such matrices are conjectured to exist whenever n = 2 or n is a multiple of 4 (see [29a, Ch. 14]).

Clearly H_n remains Hadamard if any row or column is multiplied by -1. Thus we may suppose that H_n is **normalized** so that the entries in the first row and column are equal to +1. Then every row after the first must contain $(1/2)n$ -1's and any two distinct rows after the first have $(1/4)m$ -1's in common.

A **Hadamard code** is obtained by taking the rows of H_n and of $-H_n$, and replacing +1's by 0's and -1's by 1's. This is an $(n,2n,(1/2)n)$ code.
E.g., $H_2 = \begin{pmatrix} 1 & 1 \\ 1 & -1 \end{pmatrix}$ gives the (2,4,1) code 00,01,10,11. $H_4 = \begin{pmatrix} H_2 & H_2 \\ H_2 & -H_2 \end{pmatrix}$,
$H_8 = \begin{pmatrix} H_4 & H_4 \\ H_4 & -H_4 \end{pmatrix}$, and from H_8 we obtain an (8,16,4) code:

(1.1.8)

(Note : by deleting the first column we obtain another version of the (7,16,3) Hamming code).

```
00000000
01010101
00110011
01100110
00001111
01011010
00111100
01101001
11111111
10101010
11001100
10011001
11110000
10100101
11000011
10010110
```

(1.1.9) Codes from Projective Planes

A **projective plane** [30a] is an (abstract) set of points and lines, with an incidence relation between them, satisfying three conditions:

(i)   there is a unique line through any two distinct points,

(ii)   any two distinct lines meet in a unique point,

(iii)   there are four points, no three of which are collinear.

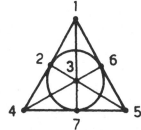

(1.1.10) E.g., A projective plane with 7 points and 7 lines:

It is easy to show that if a projective plane contains only a finite number of points, then there is an integer n such that the plane contains exactly $n^2 + n + 1$ points and $n^2 + n + 1$ lines, there are $n + 1$ points on each line, and $n + 1$ lines pass through each point. Such a plane is said to be of **order n.** The above figure shows a plane of order 2.

A projective plane of order n is known to exist whenever n is a power of a prime (2,3,4,5,7,8,9,11,13,16,17,19,...), and does not exist if $n \equiv 1$ or 2 (modulo 4) and is not of the form $a^2 + b^2$. So orders 6,14,21,... do not exist. The remaining orders (10,12,15,18,20,...) are undecided.

Suppose a projective plane of order n exists. Let $\mathcal{H}(p, \ell) = 1$ if the point p is on the line ℓ, and $= 0$ if p is not on ℓ. Then the $(n^2 + n + 1) \times (n^2 + n + 1)$ matrix $\mathcal{H} = (\mathcal{H}(p, \ell))$ is the incidence matrix of the plane.

The **projective plane code** $\mathcal{P}_n$ consists of all linear combinations (modulo 2) of the rows of $\mathcal{H}$. For example, for (1.1.10),

$$
\mathcal{H} \;=\; \begin{array}{c} \\ 1 \\ 2 \\ 3 \\ 4 \\ 5 \\ 6 \\ 7 \end{array}
\begin{array}{c} 1\;2\;3\;4\;5\;6\;7 \\ \left(\begin{array}{ccccccc}
1 & 1 & 0 & 1 & 0 & 0 & 0 \\
0 & 1 & 1 & 0 & 1 & 0 & 0 \\
0 & 0 & 1 & 1 & 0 & 1 & 0 \\
0 & 0 & 0 & 1 & 1 & 0 & 1 \\
1 & 0 & 0 & 0 & 1 & 1 & 0 \\
0 & 1 & 0 & 0 & 0 & 1 & 1 \\
1 & 0 & 1 & 0 & 0 & 0 & 1
\end{array}\right) \end{array}
\qquad (1.1.11)
$$

and the code $\mathcal{P}_2$ generated by the rows of $\mathcal{H}$ is again the Hamming code (1.1.5).

In general we have the following result.

(1.1.12) **Theorem** (Assmus and Mattson [22a])

(a) If n is odd, $\mathscr{P}_n$ is an $(n^2 + n + 1, 2^{n^2+n}, 2)$ code.

(b) If $n \equiv 2$ (modulo 4), $\mathscr{P}_n$ is an $(n^2 + n + 1,\ 2^{(n^2+n+2)/2},\ n + 1)$ code.

The code $\mathscr{P}_{10}$ has been studied in [37a].

§ 1.2 How Codes are Used

The main use for codes is to correct errors on noisy communication channels, as follows. We wish to send binary data (a stream of 0's and 1's) through a noisy channel, as fast and as reliably as possible. The channel might be a telephone line, a high frequency radio link, a satellite communication link, or a magnetic tape or disc. Because of human error, thermal noise, lightning, impulse noise, crosstalk, noise on the reading and writing heads of the tape, etc., errors occur, and the binary data received at the output of the channel is different from the transmitted data.

To put it another way, think of a telegraph line with a little old man at each end. One of them is sending 0's and 1's with a telegraph key, and the other is receiving them. The line is noisy and the little old men are deaf. The problem is to send a lot of reliable information down this line, as quickly as possible.

In order to be able to correct these errors, we **encode** the data:

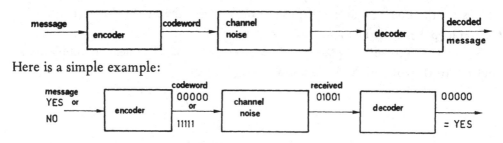

Here is a simple example:

Here 2 errors have occurred, and the decoder has decoded 01001 as the **nearest** codeword, which is 00000 or YES.

To give more precise description, we must make some assumptions about the channel. We assume the simplest possible channel, the **binary symmetric channel.** Each digit (0 or 1) is transmitted incorrectly with probability $p < 1/2$, and correctly with probability $1 - p > 1/2$. The channel has no memory from one digit to the next (Fig. 1.2.2).

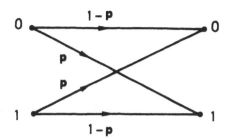

Figure 1.2.2
Binary Symmetric Channel

Suppose we are using an (n,M,d) code C containing codewords $x^{(1)}$, $x^{(2)}$, ..., $x^{(M)}$, and these codewords are all equally likely to be used. If $x^{(i)}$ is transmitted and y is received, then the best decoding strategy, known as **maximum likelihood decoding** is to decode y as that $x^{(j)}$ which maximizes

Prob{y was received $|x^{(j)}$ was transmitted}.

If y and $x^{(j)}$ differ in r places and agree in n-r places, this probability is equal to

$$p^r (1-p)^{n-r}$$

Since $p < 1/2$, this quantity is maximized if r is minimized. Thus we have the **Decoding Rule**

Decode y as that codeword $x^{(j)}$ which differs from y in the fewest places.

(1.2.3) **Definition.** The **(Hamming) distance** between two vectors x, y is the number of places where they differ.

E.g. dist(00000,01001) = 2
dist(011,101) = 2

(1.2.4) **Definition.** The **weight** wt(x) of a vector $x = (x_1,...,x_n)$ is the number of nonzero components x_i.

E.g. wt(1010101) = 4
A useful property is the obvious

(1.2.5) **Fact.** dist(x,y) = wt(x-y)

E.g. dist(1011001,0101111) = wt (1110110) = 5.

We can restate the decoding rule as:

(1.2.6)   Decode y as the closest codeword $x^{(j)}$

(Closest in the sense of Hamming distance)

This is called **nearest neighbor decoding.**

If the distance between any two codewords is at least 5, and no more than two errors occur, the receiving vector is still closer to the original codeword than any other codeword (as in Fig. 1.2.1). Thus a code with minimum distance 5 between codewords can correct $\leqslant 2$ errors. More generally, we have

(1.2.7) **Theorem.** An (n,M,d) code can correct $\leqslant [\,(d-1)/2]$ errors. (Here $[x]$ denotes the greatest integer $\leqslant x$.)

So a good code has a **small** n (for speed), a **large** M (for efficiency), and a **large** d (to correct many errors). These are conflicting aims.

The **coding theory problem** is: given n and d, to find a code with the greatest possible M. (Alternatively, given n and M, to find a code with the greatest d, etc.) For practical purposes one also wants a code which can be easily encoded and decoded.

§ 1.3 Results

In 1948 Shannon [47] proved the most important result in coding theory, the noisy channel coding theorem. For the binary symmetric channel (Fig. 1.2.2) this says the following. Associated with the channel is a quantity $C(p) = 1 + p \log p + (1-p) \log (1-p)$ called its capacity, where p is the error probability of the channel (see Fig. 1.3.1). Then for any $R < C(p)$ and any $\epsilon > 0$ there exists a code of sufficiently large block length n and rate R, having error probability less than ϵ .

It is more convenient to describe a code by its minimum distance d than by its error

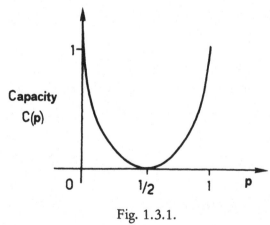

Fig. 1.3.1.

probability. Upper bounds on d in terms of n and M applying to all codes have been given by Hamming [30], Plotkin [43], Elias [48], Johnson [31] − [34], Delsarte [23], McEliece [41], and others. Lower bounds on the minimum distance of the best codes (showing that good codes exist) have been given by Gilbert [24] and Varshamov [49]. Fig. 1.3.2 is a sketch of the Elias upper bound and the Gilbert lower bound when n is large. Very recently V.I. Levenshtein has announced a new upper bound which improves on the Elias bound, but details of this result are not yet available.

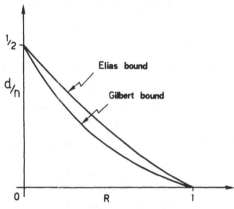

Fig. 1.3.2. The Elias and Gilbert bounds

It is known [36a], [36b], [42a] that most linear codes meet the Gilbert bound, and also [17, p. 140] that a code chosen at random will have a low probability of error, provided we have unlimited computing power to do the encoding and decoding. However the problem of finding an explicit description of codes meeting the Gilbert bound (except for rates close to 0 or 1) is still unsolved.

On the other hand, for moderate lengths, for n ⩽ 10,000 say, many good codes are known. The principal families of codes that have been discovered so far are:

(1) Hamming codes [30],

(2) Golay codes, [25], [26],

(3) Reed-Muller codes [38], [39], [46],

(4) BCH codes [1, Ch. 7],

(5) Quadratic residue codes [1, §15.2], [2, §4.4],

(6) Goppa codes [27]-[29],

(7) The Nordstrom-Robinson, Preparata, and Kerdock codes [42], [36], [44], [45],

(8) Justesen codes [35].

We shall give more detail about some of these codes later.

In these lectures we shall only discuss one type of code (the most important) namely **binary block codes**. Here the codewords are strings of 0's and 1's of constant length.

Other important families of codes are:

(1)   Convolutional codes (These are becoming increasingly important for practical purposes. See [17] §§6.8, 6.9, [3a] Ch. 13, 14);

(2)   Codes for correcting burst noise (see [17] §6.10, [3] Ch. 10, [3a] Chs. 11, 14); and

(3)   Variable length codes (used for source coding - see [31]).

§ 1.4 Exercises

(1.4.1)   Construct codes with the following parameters:

$(n,2,n)$; $(n,2^n,1)$; $(n,2^{n-1},2)$; $(4,4,2)$; $(5,4,4)$; $(6,8,3)$; $(8,16,4)$

(1.4.2)   A ternary code has symbols from GF(3); i.e., symbols which are $0, +1$, or -1. Construct a $(4,9,3)$ ternary code.

(1.4.3)   If $u = (u_1,...,u_n)$, $v = (v_1,...,v_n)$ are arbitrary binary vectors, show that

$$wt(u+v) = wt(u) + wt(v) - 2wt(u \wedge v)$$

where $u \wedge v$ is the vector which has 1's only where both u and v do.

§ 1.5 Further Reading

Abramson [21] is a good general introduction to coding and information theory, and is very easy to read. Read Chapter 1 of Gallager [17] for a general description of the communication theory problem, and then Chs. 4,5 of Wozencraft and Jacobs [18] for more information.

For Shannon's noisy-channel coding theorem see [17] Ch. 5. An amusing history of coding theory has been given by MacWilliams [37].

§ 1.6 References

Books on coding theory:

[1]   E.R. Berlekamp, **Algebraic Coding Theory**, McGraw-Hill, New York, 1968.
         (The best book available. Excellent treatment of BCH codes.)

[2]   J.H. van Lint, **Coding Theory**, Springer Verlag, Berlin, 1971 — Lecture notes
         in mathematics, number 201. (Excellent introduction, designed for
         mathematics students.)

[3]   W.W. Peterson, **Error-Correcting Codes**, MIT Press, Cambridge, Mass., 1961.
         (A good introduction to the subject for engineers.)

[3a]   W.W. Peterson and E.J. Weldon, Jr., **Error-Correcting Codes**, Second Edition,
         MIT Press, Cambridge, Mass., 1972. (Greatly expanded version of [3].)

References [1] – [3a] are required reading for anyone seriously interested in coding
theory.

[4]   F.J. MacWilliams and N.J.A. Sloane, **Combinatorial Coding Theory**, in
         preparation. (Recommended!)

[5]   Shu Lin, **An Introduction to Error-Correcting Codes,** Prentice-Hall,
         Englewood Cliffs, New Jersey, 1970. (Another introduction for
         engineers.)

[6]   Chapter 6 of [17]. (A good short introduction to coding theory. Gives a
         better description of BCH decoding than [1].)

[7]   S.W. Golomb, editor, **Digital Communications with Space Applications**,
         Prentice-Hall, Englewood Cliffs, New Jersey, 1964.

[8]   H.B. Mann, editor, **Error Correcting Codes**, Wiley, New York 1968. ([7] &
         [8] contain a number of interesting papers on coding theory,
         especially for radar applications.)

Periodicals   The first three,

[9]   IEEE (Institute of Electrical and Electronic Engineers) **Transactions on Information Theory** (abbreviated PGIT),

[10]   **Information and Control** (abbreviated IC), and

[11]   **Problemy Peredachi Informatsii** (Russian, abbreviated PPI),
            are the main sources for papers on coding theory. Occasional articles on coding theory will be found in

[12]   **IEE Transactions on Communications** (Abbreviated PGCOM) (See in 1971).

[13]   **Discrete Mathematics** (abbreviated DM. See e.g., the special issue on coding theory, September 1972.)

[14]   **IBM Journal of Research and Development**, (abbreviated IBMJ) (See e.g., the special issue on coding theory, July 1970.)

[15]   **Bell System Technical Journal** (abbreviated BSTJ).

[16]   **Journal of Combinatorial Theory**, (abbreviated JCT).

Books on Communication Theory

There are a great number of these. Four of the best are (These all show how error-correcting codes are incorporated into communication systems.)

[17]   R.G. Gallager, **Information Theory and Reliable Communication**, Wiley, New York, 1969.

[18]   J.M. Wozencraft and I.M. Jacobs, **Principles of Communication Engineering**, Wiley, New York, 1965.

[19]   Toby Berger, **Rate Distortion Theory**, Prentice-Hall, Englewood Cliffs, New
        York, 1971.

[20]   J.J. Stiffler, **Theory of Synchronous Communications,** Prentice-Hall, 1971.

Two other important books are:

[21]   N. Abramson, **Information Theory and Coding,** McGraw-Hill, N.Y., 1963. (A
        good introduction, very easy to read.)

[22]   F. Jelinek, **Probabilistic Information Theory**, McGraw-Hill, N.Y., 1968.
        (Very thorough, advanced treatment of information theory.)

Other References Cited in § § 1

[22a] Assmus, E.F., Jr., and H.F. Mattson, Jr., (1970), The Algebraic Theory of
        Codes II, AFCRL Report 71-0013, especially Part II.

[23] Delsarte, P. (1972), Bounds for Unrestricted Codes, by Linear Programming,
        PRR 27: 272-289.

[24] Gilbert, E.N. (1952), A Comparison of Signalling Alphabets, BSTJ 39:
        1253-2156.

[25] Golay, M.J.E. (1949), Notes on Digital Coding, PIEEE 37: 657.

[26] Golay, M.J.E. (1954), Binary Coding, PGIT 4: 23-28.

[27] Goppa, V.D. (1970), A New Class of Linear Error-Correcting Codes, PPI
        6(3): 24-30.

[28] Goppa, V.D. (1971), Rational Representation of Codes and (L,G) Codes, PPI
        7(3): 41-49.

[29] Goppa, V.D. (1972), Some Codes Constructed on the Basis of (L,G) Codes,
        PPI 8(2): 107-109.

[29a] Hall, M., Jr. (1967), Combinatorial Theory, Balisdell, Watham, Mass.

[30] Hamming, R.W. (1950), Error Detecting and Error Correcting Codes, BSTJ
       29: 147-160.

[30a] Hughes, D.R. and F.C. Piper (1973), Projective Planes, Springer, New
       York.

[31] Johnson, S.M. (1962), A New Upper Bound for Error-Correcting Codes,
       PGIT 8: 203-207.

[32] Johnson, S.M. (1963), Improved Asymptotic Bounds for Error-Correcting
       Codes, PGIT 9: 198-205.

[33] Johnson, S.M. (1971), On Upper Bounds for Unrestricted Binary Error-
       Correcting Codes, PGIT 17: 466-478.

[34] Johnson, S.M. (1972), Upper Bounds for Constant Weight Error-Correcting
       Codes, DM 3: 109-124.

[35] Justesen, J. (1972), A Class of Constructive Asymptotically Good
       Algebraic Codes, PGIT 18: 652-656.

[36] Kerdock, A.M. (1972), A Class of Low-rate Nonlinear Binary Codes, IC
       20: 182-187.

[36a] Koshelev, V.N. (1965), Some Properties of Random Group Codes of Large
       Length, PPI 1: 45-48.

[36b] Kozlov, M.V. (1969), The Correcting Capacities of Linear Codes, Soviet
       Physics – Doklady 14: 413-415.

[37] MacWilliams, F.J., N.J.A. Sloane, and J.G. Thompson (1973), On The
       Existence of a Projective Plane of Order 10, JCT 14A: 66-78.

[38] Mitani, N. (1951), On the Transmission of Numbers in a Sequential
       Computer, Delivered at the National Convention of the Inst. of
       Elect. Engineers of Japan, November 1951.

[39] Müller, D.E. (1954), Application of Boolean Algebra to Switching Circuit
       Design and to Error Detection, PGEC 3: 6-12.

[40] Mykkeltveit, J. (1972), A Note on Kerdock Codes, JPL Report 32-1526,
       Vol. 9: 82-83.

[41] Mykkeltveit, J., C. Lam and R. J. McEliece (1973), On the Weight
       Enumerators of Quadratic Residue Codes, JPL Report 32-1526.

[42] Nordstrom, A.W. and J.P. Robinson (1967), An Optimum Nonlinear Code,
       IC 11: 613-616.

[42a] Pierce, J.N. (1967), Limit Distribution of the Minimum Distance of
       Random Linear Codes, PGIT 13: 595-599.

[43] Plotkin, M. (1960), Binary Codes with Specified Minimum Distances,
       PGIT 6: 445-450.

[44] Preparata, F.P. (1968), A Class of Optimum Nonlinear Double-Error-
       Correcting Codes, IC 13: 378-400.

[45] Preparata,   F.P.   (1968A),   Weight   and   Distances   Structure   of
       Nordstrom-Robinson Quadratic Code, IC 12: 466–473 and 13: 172.

[46] Reed, I.S. (1954), A Class of Multiple-Error-Correcting Codes and the
       Decoding Scheme, PGIT 4: 38-49.

[47]   Shannon, C.E. (1948), A Mathematical Theory of Communication, BSTJ 27:
       379-423 and 623-656. Reprinted in **A Mathematical Theory of
       Communication,** by C.E. Shannon and W. Weaver, University of
       Illinois Press, Urbana, Illinois, 1963.

[48] Shannon, C.E., R.G. Gallager, and E.R. Berlekamp (1967), Lower Bounds Error Probability for Coding on Discrete Memory Channels, IC 10: 65-103 and 522-552.

[49] Varshamov, R.R. (1957), Estimate of the Number of Signals in Error-Correcting Codes, Dokl. Akad. Nauk SSSR, 117: 739-741.

Abbreviations of Journals used in these Lectures

AFCRC	=	AIR FORCE CAMBRIDGE RESEARCH CENTER, BEDFORD, MASS.
AFCRL	=	AIR FORCE CAMBRIDGE RESEARCH LABORATORIES HANSCOM FIELD, MASS.
AMM	=	AMERICAN MATHEMATICAL MONTHLY.
AMS	=	ANNALS OF MATHEMATICAL STATISTICS.
BAMS	=	BULLETIN OF THE AMERICAN MATHEMATICAL SOCIETY.
BSTJ	=	BELL SYSTEM TECHNICAL JOURNAL.
CJM	=	CANADIAN JOURNAL OF MATHEMATICS.
DM	=	DISCRETE MATHEMATICS.
IBMJ	=	IBM JOURNAL OF RESEARCH AND DEVELOPMENT.
IC	=	INFORMATION AND CONTROL
IECEJ	=	INSTITUTE OF ELECTRONICS AND COMMUNICATION ENGINEERS OF JAPAN (JAPANESE).
JPL	=	JET PROPULSION LABORATORY OF CALIFORNIA INSTITUTE OF TECHNOLOGY, PASADENA, CALIFORNIA.
MTAC	=	MATHEMATICS OF COMPUTATION (FORMERLY MATHEMATICAL TABLES AND OTHER AIDS TO COMPUTATION).
NYAS	=	ANNALS OF NEW YORK ACADEMY OF SCIENCES.
PGCOM	=	IEEE TRANSACTIONS ON COMMUNICATION TECHNOLOGY
PGEC	=	IEEE TRANSACTIONS ON COMPUTERS (FORMERLY IEEE TRANSACTIONS ON ELECTRONIC COMPUTERS).
PGIT	=	IEEE TRANSACTIONS ON INFORMATION THEORY
PIEEE	=	PROCEEDINGS IEEE.
PRI	=	PROBLEMY PEREDACHI INFORMATSII (RUSSIAN).
PRR	=	PHILLIPS RESEARCH REPORTS.
SIAMJ	=	SIAM JOURNAL ON APPLIED MATHEMATICS.
SIAMR	=	SIAM REVIEW.

§§ 2 Linear Codes

§ 2.1 Introduction

To make codes easier to use and to analyze we must impose some algebraic structure on them. The simplest assumption is that the code is linear. In this chapter we give the basic theory of linear codes, including the fundamental notions of generator matrix, parity check matrix, dual code, and standard decoding array.

§ 2.2 Definition of Linear Code

Almost all the codes discussed in these lectures are binary codes. That is, they have symbols from the field $F = GF(2) = \{0,1\}$. In this field $1 + 1 = 0$, $+1 = -1$. Elements of F are called **bits**. F^n denotes the n-dimensional vector space consisting of all binary vectors of length n.

(1.1.1) says that a code is any subset of F^n. Sometimes it is helpful to think of F^n as the vertices of a unit n-dimensional cube -see Fig. 2.2.1.

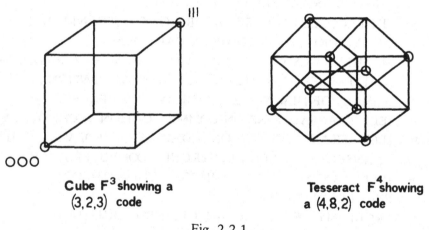

Cube F^3 showing a
(3,2,3) code

Tesseract F^4 showing
a (4,8,2) code

Fig. 2.2.1.

Then the coding theory problem is to pick M vertices of the cube as far apart from each other as possible. (**Aside:** The corresponding problem of placing M points on the surface of a unit **sphere** in n-dimensions is also of fundamental importance for communication theory, and is also unsolved. See Wyner [57], [58] and Slepian [55].)

(2.2.2) **Definition** A **linear code** $\mathscr{C}$ is a linear subspace of F^n.

Equivalently: A (binary) code is linear if the sum of any two codewords is a codeword.

Examples: The codes $(1.2.2) - (1.1.5)$ are linear but $(1.1.6)$ is not.

Let us pick a maximal set of linearly independent codewords of $\mathscr{C}$, say $x^{(1)}, \ldots, x^{(k)}$. Then $\mathscr{C}$ consists of all 2^k linear combinations

$$a_1 x^{(1)} + \ldots + a_k x^{(k)}, \quad a_i \in F.$$

The $k \times n$ binary matrix

$$G = \begin{pmatrix} x^{(1)} \\ \vdots \\ x^{(k)} \end{pmatrix}$$

is called a **generator matrix** for the code. The code is the row space of G.

(2.2.3) E.g. Generator matrices for the codes $(1.1.2) - (1.1.5)$ are:

$$(11111), \qquad \begin{pmatrix} 011 \\ 101 \end{pmatrix}$$

$$\begin{pmatrix} 1110100 \\ 0111010 \\ 0011101 \end{pmatrix} \text{ and } \begin{pmatrix} 1110100 \\ 0111010 \\ 0011101 \\ 1111111 \end{pmatrix}$$

(2.2.4) **Theorem** Every linear $(n, 2^k, d)$ code has a generator matrix which is a binary $(k \times n)$ matrix of rank k; and conversely every such matrix is the generator matrix of a code.

Notation A linear $(n, 2^k, d)$ code will be described as an $[n, k, d]$ or $[n, k]$ code.

Definition Two codes which differ only in the order of their coordinates are said to be **equivalent**. Obviously equivalent codes can correct exactly the same number of errors, although there may be very good engineering reasons for preferring one form to another.

E.g.
$$\begin{array}{ll} 0000 & 0000 \\ 0011 \text{ and } 0101 \\ 1100 & 1010 \\ 1111 & 1111 \end{array}$$
are equivalent $(4,4,2)$ codes.

(2.2.5) **Unsolved Problem**

Many $(k \times n)$ generator matrices generate equivalent codes. In 1960 [54] counted inequivalent [n,k] codes using Pólya's counting method. But the number of inequivalent [n,k] codes having a given minimum distance d remains unsolved. MacWilliams, Sloane, and Thompson [53] have made a little progress on this problem.

Canonical Form for Generator Matrix

By possibly choosing a different set of generators and rearranging the order of the coordinates, we can put the generator matrix into the **canonical form**

$$G = \left[I \vdots A \right]$$

where I is a $k \times k$ unit matrix and $A = (a_{ij})$ is an arbitrary $k \times (n-k)$ binary matrix. E.g. Canonical forms for (2.2.3) are

$$(11111), \quad \begin{pmatrix} 101 \\ 011 \end{pmatrix}, \quad \begin{pmatrix} 1000111 \\ 0101011 \\ 0011101 \end{pmatrix}, \quad \begin{pmatrix} 10001001 \\ 01000101 \\ 00100011 \\ 00011110 \end{pmatrix} .$$

Exercise: Find generator matrices for the [n,1,n] repetition and [n,n-1,2] even weight codes.

§ 2.3 Encoding

Suppose the message to be encoded is

$$\underset{\sim}{u} = (u_1, \ldots, u_k) \quad u_i \in F.$$

The corresponding codeword $\underset{\sim}{x}$ is simply found (in theory) by multiplying by the canonical generator matrix:

$$\underset{\sim}{x} = \underset{\sim}{u} G$$

$$= (x_1, \ldots, x_k, x_{k+1}, \ldots, x_n) \qquad (2.3.1)$$

where

$$x_i = c_i, \quad 1 \leqslant i \leqslant k$$

are the **message bits**, and

$$x_{k+i} = \sum_{j=1}^{k} a_{ji} x_j \quad 1 \leqslant i \leqslant n-k \qquad (2.3.1a)$$

are the **check bits**. These represent **redundancy** which has been added to the message to give protection against noise. This explains why

$$R = \frac{\log_2 M}{n} = \frac{k}{n}$$

is called the **rate** or **efficiency** of an [n,k] code.

The **parity chek matrix** of the code is

$$H = \left[-A^T \vdots I \right]_{(n-k) \times n}$$

where I is an (n-k) x (n-k) unit matrix.

Note that

$$GH^T = 0 \qquad (2.3.2)$$

Each row vector $\underline{h}$ of H is therefore orthogonal to every codeword $\underline{x}$:

$$\underline{x} \cdot \underline{h} = \sum_{i=1}^{n} x_i h_i = 0, \; \forall \, \underline{x} \in \text{ code} \qquad (2.3.3)$$

Thus the rows of H are **parity checks** on the codewords — they say that certain coordinates in each codeword must sum to zero.

Let r = n-k. Then r is the number of linearly independent parity checks on the code, or the number of check symbols in each codeword.

We could use (2.3.3) as a definition of the code. Alternatively, the code is the null space of the rows of H.

(2.3.4) **Definition** If $\mathscr{C}$ is a linear [n,k] code, then the **dual code** $\mathscr{C}^\perp$ is

$$\mathscr{C}^\perp = \left\{ \underline{u} \mid \underline{u} \cdot \underline{v} = 0, \ \forall v \in \mathscr{C} \right\} .$$

Clearly $\mathscr{C}^\perp$ is the orthogonal subspace to $\mathscr{C}$ and is an [n,n-k] linear code. If $\mathscr{C} = \mathscr{C}^\perp$ it is said to be **self-dual** (Example: {00,11} is self-dual).

(The minimum distance of $\mathscr{C}^\perp$ will be discussed in §§4.2.) From (2.3.2) we have:

(2.3.5) **Theorem**

If $G = [I,A]$ is the generator matrix for $\mathscr{C}$, then $H = [-A^T, I]$ is the generator matrix for $\mathscr{C}^\perp$.

Examples.

The dual of (1.1.2) is the [5,4,2] **even weight** code (consisting of all codewords with an even number of 1's.) The dual of (1.1.3) is {000, 111}. (1.1.4) and (1.1.5) are duals of each other. (1.1.6) is not linear and so does not have a dual. (But it is possible to define the dual of nonlinear code so that (1.1.6) is its own dual! See MacWilliams, Sloane and Geothals [52], and also [4]).

The minimum distance d between the codewords of a linear code $\mathscr{C}$ is

$$d = \min_{u, \ v \in \mathscr{C}} \text{dist} \ (u,v)$$

by (1.2.5)
$$= \min_{u, \ v \in \mathscr{C}} \text{wt} \ (u + v)$$

(2.3.6)
$$= \min_{\substack{u \in \mathscr{C} \\ u \neq 0}} \text{wt} \ (u),$$

since the code is closed under addition. Without this property it is much harder to find d.

A theorem with many applications in coding theory and combinatorics is:

(2.3.7) **Theorem** If $\mathscr{C}$ is an [n,k,d] linear code, then its parity check matrix is a (n-k)xn binary matrix in which any d-1 or fewer columns are linearly independent over GF(2).

Proof. If λ columns of H sum to zero then there is a codeword of weight λ in $\mathscr{C}$.

§ 2.4 Decoding

Suppose the codeword $\underline{x} = (x_1,...,x_n)$ is transmitted, the channel adds a noise vector $\underline{e} = (e_1,...,e_n)$, and the vector $\underline{y} = \underline{x} + \underline{e}$ is received.

$$\underline{x} = (x_1, ... , x_n) \longrightarrow \oplus \longrightarrow \underline{y} = (y_1, ... , y_n)$$
$$\underline{e} = (e_1, ... , e_n)$$

Given $\underline{y}$, according to our decoding rule (1.2.6), the decoder must find the closest codeword $\underline{x}$, or equivalently the error vector of smallest weight.

Now the linear [n,k,d] code $\mathscr{C}$ is a subgroup of F^n, so we may partition F^n into cosets of $\mathscr{C}$:

$$F = \mathscr{C} \cup (\underline{a}_1 + \mathscr{C}) \cup ... \cup (\underline{a}_t + \mathscr{C}), \qquad (2.4.1)$$

where

$$t = 2^{n-k} - 1.$$

Suppose $\underline{y} \in \underline{a}_i + \mathscr{C}$. Then the only possible error patterns $\underline{e}$ are exactly the elements of the coset $\underline{a}_i + \mathscr{C}$. The decoder therefore must choose a minimum weight element $\underline{e}_i$ in the coset, called the **coset representative**, and decode $\underline{y}$ as $\underline{x} = \underline{y} + \underline{e}_i$.

There is a nice way of describing this process, invented by Slepian, and called the **Standard Array** for the code. The first row of the array is the code, and the other rows are the cosets. The left hand element in each coset is the coset representative.

(2.4.2) Example of a standard array:

$$G = \begin{pmatrix} 1010 \\ 0101 \end{pmatrix} = \text{generator matrix}$$

	Syndrome				
code →	0000	1010	0101	1111	00
	1000	0010	1101	0111	10
	0100	1110	0001	1011	01
	1100	0110	1001	0011	11

Coset
representatives

When $\underline{y}$ is received, it is decoded as the codeword at the top of the column containing $\underline{y}$. E.g., 1101 would be decoded as 0101, which assumes that $\underline{e}$ = 1000.

The coset representatives in the left-hand column are the error patterns which are corrected. Then the probability that the decoder does decode correctly is the probability that the error pattern is one of these cosets representatives. If there are α_i coset representatives of weight i, then:

(2.4.2) **Theorem**

Probability of correct decoding =

$$\sum_{i=0}^{n} \alpha_i \ p^i \ (1 - p)^{n-i} .$$

(2.4.3) **Unsolved Problem**

Calculate this probability for any of the known families of codes!

Even for the extremely simple family of first-order Reed Muller codes, the α_i 's are only known up to length 64 – see Sloane & Dick [56], Berlekamp and Welch [50a], and Sarwate (unpublished). The α_i's for these codes are also important for studying the behaviour of Hadamard transforms – see Berlekamp [50].

Rothaus (unpublished) has studied the greatest possible weight of a coset representative of a first-order Reed Müller code, but even this is not solved yet.

Hobbs [51] and Sloane & Dick [56] have given approximations to the α_i.

(2.4.4) The **syndrome** s of y is given by

$$s^T \ = \ Hy^T .$$

Thus s is a binary vector of length r = n-k. Since

$$s^T = Hy^T = H(x^T + e^T) = He^T \, , \qquad (2.4.5)$$

vectors in the same coset have the same syndrome, and conversely. Hence:

(2.4.6) **Theorem** There is a 1-1 correspondence between syndromes and cosets. (Example: see (2.4.2)).

I.e., the syndrome tells you which coset $\underline{y}$ is in. Then simply add the coset representative to do the decoding.

From (2.4.5) we have the important:

(2.4.7) **Theorem** The (transposed) syndrome is equal to the sum of the columns of H where the errors occurred.

§ 2.5 Further Reading

Most of this material is standard and can be found for example in [1] § 1.1, [3] Ch. 3. etc. For applications of Th. (2.3.7) to document retrieval and to combinatorics see [50b], [50c].

§ 2.6 References

[50] Berlekamp, E.R., (1970) Some mathematical properties of a scheme for reducing the bandwidth of motion pictures by Hadamard smearing, BSTJ 49: 969-986.

[50a] Berlekamp, E.R. and L.R. Welch (1972), Weight distributions of the cosets of the (32,6) Reed-Müller code, PGIT 18: 203-207.

[50b] Chien, R.T., and W.D. Frazer (1966), An application of coding theory to document retrieval, PGIT 12: 92-96.

[50c] Gulati, B.R. (1972), More about maximal (n,r)-sets, IC 20: 188-191.

[51]   Hobbs, C.F. (1965), Approximating the performance of a binary group code, PGIT 11: 142-144.

[52]   MacWilliams, F.J., N.J.A. Sloane, and J.M. Goethals (1972), The MacWilliams identities for nonlinear codes, BSTJ 51: 803-819.

[53]   Mac Williams, F.J., N.J.A. Sloane and J.G. Thompson (1972), Good self dual codes exist, DM 3: 153-162.

[54]   Slepian, D. (1960), Some further theory of group codes, BSTJ 39: 1219-1252.

[55]   Slepian, D. (1968), Group codes for the Gaussian channel, BSTJ 47: 575-602.

[56]   Sloane, N.J.A. and R.J. Dick (1971), On the enumeration of cosets of first order Reed-Müller codes, IEEE Intern, Conf. on Commun., Montreal 1971, 7: 36-2 to 36-6.

[57]   Wyner, A.D. (1965A), Capabilities of bounded discrepancy decoding, BSTJ
        44: 1061-1122.

[58]   Wyner, A.D. (1969), On coding and information theory, SIAMR 11:
        317-346.

§§ 3 The Golay Code

§ 3.1 Introduction

In this chapter we describe one of the most important of all codes, the [24,12,8] extended Golay code.

§ 3.2 Weight Distribution of a Code

The **weight** wt(u) of a vector $u = (u_1,...,u_n)$ is the number of nonzero u_i. The first thing one wants to know about a linear code is its minimum nonzero weight, for by (2.3.6) this is the minimum distance between codewords, and so, by (1.2.7), determines the number of errors the code can correct.

The next most important property of a code is its **weight distribution**, i.e., the numbers A_i = number of codewords of weight i.

It is convenient to use the generating function

(3.2.1)
$$W_c(x,y) = \sum_{u \in c} x^{n-wt(u)} y^{wt(u)}$$
$$= \sum_{i=0}^{n} A_i x^{n-i} y^{i} ,$$

which we call the **weight enumerator** of c.

E.g. The weight enumerators of the codes (1.1.2) − (1.1.5) are $x^5 + y^5$; $x^3 + 3xy^2$; $x^7 + 7x^3 y^4$; and $x^7 + 7x^4 7^3 + 7x^3 y^4 + y^7$, respectively.

It is useful to have W as a homogeneous polynomial of degree n. But of course we can put x = 1 to get

$$W_c(y) = \sum_{i=0}^{n} A_i y^{i}$$

Finding the weight enumerator of a large code is in general very difficult.

§ 3.3 Extending a Code

(3.3.1) **Lemma** Let c be any (n,M,d) code with d odd. By adding a 0 at the end of each codeword of even weight, and a 1 at the end of each codeword of odd weight, we obtain a new (n+1,M,d+1) code c'.

Proof. From (1.4.3), the distance between any two vectors of c' is even. The minimum distance cannot be less than d (which is odd), so must be d + 1. Q.E.D.

This technique is called **extending** the code by adding an **overall parity check** (for now the codewords satisfy the additional constraint that $\sum_{i=1}^{n} x_i = 0$).

Adding an overall parity check to (1.1.5) we obtain the (8,16,4) **extended Hamming code**. Its weight enumerator is

$$\varphi_2(x,y) \overset{\Delta}{=} x^8 + 14x^4 y^4 + y^8 \qquad (3.3.2)$$

The infinite family of Hamming codes will be defined in §§ 5.8.

§ 3.4 The [24,12,8] Extended Golay Code and Its Properties

The Golay code is probably the most important of all codes. In this section we give an elementary definition of the code, and establish a number of its properties. (This code may also be defined as a quadratic residue code, as a BCH code, and [79a] by combining two versions of the (8,16,4) extended Hamming code.)

(3.4.1) **Definition** The extended Golay code $\mathscr{G}$ has generator matrix:

G =

	∞	0	1	2	3	4	5	6	7	8	9	10	∞	0	1	2	3	4	5	6	7	8	9	10
	1	1												1	1		1	1	1				1	
	1		1												1	1		1	1	1				1
	1			1										1		1	1		1	1	1			
	1				1										1		1	1		1	1	1		
	1					1										1		1	1		1	1	1	
	1						1										1		1	1		1	1	1
	1							1						1				1		1	1		1	1
	1								1					1	1				1		1	1		1
	1									1				1	1	1				1		1	1	
	1										1				1	1	1				1		1	1
	1											1		1		1	1	1				1		1
													1	1	1	1	1	1	1	1	1	1	1	1

(The columns are labelled $\ell_\infty \ell_0 \ell_1 \dots \ell_{10}\, r_\infty r_0 \dots r_{10}$.)

(3.4.2) **Theorem** $\mathscr{G}$ has the following properties:

(3.4.3) $\mathscr{G}$ is a $[24,12,8]$ code;

(3.4.4) $\mathscr{G}$ is self-dual: $\mathscr{G} = \mathscr{G}^{\perp}$;

(3.4.5) the weight of every codeword is a multiple of 4;

(3.4.6) $\underline{1} \in \mathscr{G}$

(3.4.7) $\mathscr{G}$ is invariant under the permutation of coordinates

$$T = (\ell_{\infty} r_{\infty}) (\ell_0 r_0) (\ell_1 r_{10}) (\ell_2 r_9) \dots (\ell_{10} r_1) ,$$

which interchanges the two halves of a codeword.

(3.4.8) $\mathscr{G}$ has the weight distribution:

i	:	0	8	12	16	24
A_i	:	1	759	2576	759	1

and weight enumerator

(3.4.9) $\varphi_3 (x,y) = x^{24} + 759 x^{16} y^8 + 2576 x^{12} y^{12} + 759 x^8 y^{16} + y^{24}$

Proof (i) Let A be the 11 x 11 circulant matrix on the right of G. The first row has 1's at the quadratic residues $0,1,2 = 4$, $3 = 9$, $4 = 5$, $5 = 3$ modulo 11. $\mathscr{G}$ clearly has dimension 12.

(3.4.10) If u,v are two distinct rows of A, then $\text{wt}(u \cap v) = 3$. (It is sufficient to check this when u is the first row.) Therefore $\text{wt}(u+v) = 6$.

(ii) Hence if u,v are any two (not necessarily distinct) rows of G, then $\text{wt}(u \cap v) \equiv 0$ (modulo 2). I.e., $u \cdot v = 0$. This implies that $\mathscr{G} \subseteq \mathscr{G}^{\perp}$. Therefore $\mathscr{G} = \mathscr{G}^{\perp}$ by (i).

(iii) The weight of every row of G is a multiple of 4. Then (ii) and

$$\text{wt}(u + v) = \text{wt}(u) + \text{wt}(v) - 2\text{wt}(u \cap v)$$

imply that every codeword has weigth divisible by 4.

(iv) The sum of the rows of G is $\underline{1}$.

(v) To show that $\mathscr{G}$ is invariant under T: T sends the first row of G into

$$0,1,0100011101,1,1,0000000000$$

which is easily verified to be the sum of rows 0,2,6,7,8,10,11, and therefore is in the code. T sends the last row of G into $1^{12}\,0^{12}$, which is the complement of the last row, and is in the code by (iv).

(vi) We divide each vector of $\mathscr{G}$ into a left half L and a right half R. Clearly wt(L) $\equiv$ wt(R) $\equiv 0$ (modulo 2). $\bar{R}$ will denote the complement of the right half.

(vii) $\mathscr{G}$ contains no vector of weight 4. To prove this, by (3.4.7) we may suppose that a vector of weight 4 is of one of the types

$$(1)\ \ \text{wt(L)} = 0,\ \text{wt(R)} = 4;\ \ (2)\ \ \text{wt(L)} = 2,\ \text{wt(R)} = 2.$$

(1) is impossible, since if wt(L) = 0, wt(R) = 0 or 12.
(2) is impossible, since if wt(L) = 2, L is the sum of one or two rows of G, plus possibly the last row. In each case wt(R) = 6 by (i).

(viii) Thus the weighs occurring in $\mathscr{G}$ are 0,8,12,16,24. Let A_i be the number of words of weight i. Then $A_0 = A_{24} = 1$, $A_8 = A_{16}$. To each left hand side L there are two possible right hand sides, R and $\bar{R}$. We can now list all the vectors in $\mathscr{G}$:

Number	wt(L)	wt(R)	wt($\bar{R}$)	Total weight	
1	0	0	12	0	12
$11 + \binom{11}{2}$	2	6	6	8	8
$\binom{11}{3} + \binom{11}{4}$	4	4	8	8	12
α = ?	6	2	10	8	16
β = ?	6	6	6	12	12
$\binom{11}{7} + \binom{11}{8}$	8	4	8	12	16
$\binom{11}{9} + \binom{11}{10}$	10	6	6	16	16
1	12	0	12	12	24

But by (3.4.7), α is equal to the number of vectors of type (2,6), which is $2(11 + \binom{11}{2})$. Therefore

$$A_8 = 4 \left(11 + \binom{11}{2}\right) + \binom{11}{3} + \binom{11}{4} = 759$$

and so $A_{12} = 2576$.   QED.

(3.4.11) **Theorem** Any vector of weight 5 in F^{24} is contained in exactly one codeword of $\mathscr{G}$ of weight 8. Proof. If a vector of weight 5 were contained in two codewords u,v of weight 8, then dist(u,v) $\leqslant$ 6, a contradiction. So each codeword of weight 8 contains $\binom{8}{5}$ vectors of weight 5, which are all distinct, and

$$759 \binom{8}{5} = \binom{24}{5} \qquad \text{QED}$$

(3.4.12) **Definition** A t-(v,k,λ) design in a set of binary vectors (called **blocks**) of length v and weight k, such that any vector of weight t is contained in exactly λ blocks. Such a set is also called a **t-design**, or a tactical configuration.

For example, the codewords of weight 3 in the (7,16,3) code of example (1.1.5) form a 2-(7,3,1) design.

```
1 1 0 1 0 0 0
0 1 1 0 1 0 0
0 0 1 1 0 1 0
0 0 0 1 1 0 1
1 0 0 0 1 1 0
0 1 0 0 0 1 1
1 0 1 0 0 0 1
```

In any t-(v,k,λ) design, containing say b blocks, we write $u \subset \beta$ if a vector u of weight t is contained in a block β. By counting the pairs $u \subset \beta$ in two ways, we obtain.

(3.4.13)

$$b \binom{k}{t} = \lambda \binom{v}{t},$$

$$b = \lambda \binom{v}{t} / \binom{k}{t}$$

Theorem (3.4.11) shows that the codewords of weight 8 in the extended Golay code form a 5-(24,8,1) design.

Another proof of this result follows from Assmus and Mattson's theorem [60] (which we do not have time to prove here), which says that if a code contains weights $0, \tau_1, \tau_2, \dots, \tau_s, n$ and the dual code has minimum weight $d' > s$, then the codewords of weight τ_i form a $(d'-s)$-design, for $i = 1, \dots, s$.

This theorem, together with (3.4.8) and (3.4.13), implies

(3.4.14) Theorem The codewords of weights 8, 12, and 16 in the extended Golay code form

$$5 - (24, 8, 1)$$
$$5 - (24, 12, 48)$$
$$5 - (24, 16, 78)$$

designs, respectively.

A very useful consequence of (3.4.14) is

(3.4.15) Theorem Let u be a codeword of $\mathscr{G}$ of weight 8, with 1's in coordinates $a_1, a_2, \dots, a_8$. Then the number of codewords of weight 8 which have 1's in coordinates $a_1, \dots, a_j$ and 0's in $a_{j+1}, \dots, a_i$ ($j \leqslant i \leqslant 8$) is the $(j+1)$th entry in the $(i+1)$th line of Table (3.4.16):

Table 3.4.16

0	759							
1	506	253						
2	330	176	77					
3	210	120	56	21				
4	130	80	40	16	5			
5	78	52	28	12	4	1		
6	46	32	20	8	4	0	1	
7	30	16	16	4	4	0	0	1
8	30	0	16	0	4	0	0	0	1

(The analogous table for codewords of weight 12 is:

Table 3.4.17

0					2576				
1				1288	1288				
2				616	672	616			
3			280	336	336	280			
4		120	160	176	160	120			
5	48	72	88	88	72	48			
6	16	32	40	48	40	32	16		
7	0	16	16	24	24	16	16	0	
8	0	0	16	0	24	0	16	0	0

Proof. A 5-design is also a t-design for $t \leqslant 5$. Therefore the number of codewords of weight 8 which have 1's in coordinates $a_1,...,a_t$ is, from (3.4.13),

$$759 \binom{8}{t} \Big/ \binom{24}{t} \qquad \text{for} \quad t \leqslant 5,$$

$$1 \qquad \text{for} \quad 5 \leqslant t \leqslant 8,$$

which gives the right hand entries of the table. The remaining entries are filled in by subtraction: 506 = 759-253, etc. Similarly for the codewords of weight 12.

(3.4.18) **Exercise** In a t-(v,k,λ) design, let b be the number of blocks, and let λ_i be the number of blocks containing a fixed vector of weight i ($i \leqslant t$), so that $\lambda_t = \lambda$. Show that the Golay code gives rise to the following designs:

v	k	b	λ_1	λ_2	λ_3	λ_4	λ_5
24	8	759	253	77	21	5	1
23	7	253	77	21	5	1	
23	8	506	176	56	16	4	
22	6	77	21	5	1		
22	7	176	56	16	4		
22	8	330	120	40	12		

(3.4.19) **Exercise** Show that the 4096 cosets of $\mathcal{G}$ have the following weight distributions:

Number/Weight	0	2	4	6	8	10	12	14	16	18	20	22	24
1	1				759		2576		759				1
276		1		77	352	946	1344	946	352	77		1	
1771			6	64	360	960	1316	960	360	64	6		

Number/Weight	1	3	5	7	9	11	13	15	17	19	21	23
24	1			253	506	1288	1288	506	253			1
2024		1	21	168	640	1218	1218	640	168	21	1	

§ 3.5 Further Properties of the Golay Code

(3.5.1) **Definition** The automorphism group Aut(c) of a code c of length n consists of all permutations of the n coordinates which send codewords into codewords. Thus Aut(c) is a subgroup of the symmetric group $\mathcal{S}_n$.

(3.5.2) **Theorem** The automorphism group of the extended Golay code is the simple Mathieu group M_{24}, of order $24.23.22.21.20.16.3 = 244823040$. This group is 5-fold transitive, that is, it contains a permutation which sends any ordered set of 5 coordinates onto any other ordered set of 5 coordinates.

The proof is omitted.

(3.5.3) **Definition** The (unextended) **Golay code** $\mathcal{G}_{23}$ is obtained from $\mathcal{G}$ by deleting the last coordinate from every codeword.

(From 3.5.2, it doesn't matter which coordinate is deleted.)

(3.5.4) **Theorem** $\mathcal{G}_{23}$ is a [23,12,7] code, which can be made cyclic by a suitable permutation of the coordinates.

The proof is omitted

We shall see in § 5.10 that $\mathcal{G}_{23}$ is a perfect code.

§3.6 Encoding and Decoding the Extended Golay Code $\mathcal{G}$

Since $\mathcal{G}$ is an extended cyclic code (3.5.4), encoding is easy. (In any case, for a code of this size, the encoding could be done directly from (2.3.1).)

We shall give two decoding methods, of which the first is the more practical, the second the more elegant.

(3.6.1) **Decoding Method I** (Berlekamp [62]) Let us take the generator and parity check matrix in the canonical form (obtained from (3.4.1) by moving the left hand column to the right):

$$
G = H = \left(\begin{array}{c|c|c} I_{12} & A & \begin{matrix} 1 \\ 1 \\ \vdots \\ 1 \end{matrix} \\ \hline & 11\ldots 1 & 0 \end{array} \right) = (I_{12} \mid B)
$$

$$
= (u_1 , \ldots , u_{12} , b_{13} , \ldots , b_{24}) ,
$$

say (giving names to the columns). Thus u_i is a vector with 1 in coordinate i. $GH^T = 0$ implies $I + BB^T = 0$ or $B^{-1} = B^T$.

Also let

$$
B = \left(\begin{matrix} b_1^T \\ b_2^T \\ \ldots \\ b_{12}^T \end{matrix} \right)
$$

(giving names to the rows of B).

Suppose the codeword $x = (x_1,\ldots,x_{24})$ is transmitted, the noise vector $e = (e_1 , \ldots , e_{24})$ is added, and $y = x + e$ is received. The syndrome (2.4.4) is

(3.6.2)
$$
s^T = Hy^T = He^T
$$
$$
= \sum_{i=1}^{12} e_i u_i + \sum_{i=13}^{24} e_i b_i .
$$

Also

(3.6.3)
$$
B^T s^T = B^T He^T = [B^T \mid I] e^T
$$
$$
= \sum_{i=1}^{12} e_i b_i + \sum_{i=13}^{24} e_i u_{i-12} .
$$

Suppose that $\text{wt}(e) \leqslant 3$. Then at least one of the following conditions must hold:

Case I: $\quad \text{wt}(e_{13}, \dots, e_{24}) = 0, \ \text{wt}(S^T) \leqslant 3, \ \sum_{i=1}^{12} e_i u_i = S^T$.

Case II: $\quad \text{wt}(e_{13}, \dots, e_{24}) = 1$, so for some j, $13 \leqslant j \leqslant 24$,

$$\text{wt}(S^T + b_j) \leqslant 2 \text{ and } \sum_{i=1}^{12} e_i u_i = S^T + b_j.$$

Case III: $\quad \text{wt}(e_1, \dots, e_{12}) = 0, \ \text{wt}(B^T S^T) \leqslant 3,$

$$\sum_{i=13}^{24} e_i u_{i-12} = B^T S^T.$$

Case IV: $\quad \text{wt}(e_1, \dots, e_{12}) = 1$, so for some j, $1 \leqslant j \leqslant 12$,

$$\text{wt}(B^T S^T + b_j) \leqslant 2 \text{ and}$$

$$\sum_{i=13}^{24} e_i u_{i-12} = B^T S^T + b_j.$$

Thus the decoding can be done by computing the weights of the 26 vectors S^T, $S^T + b_j$ $(1 \leqslant j \leqslant 12)$, $B^T S^T$, $B^T S^T + b_j$ $(1 \leqslant j \leqslant 12)$.
Example: $S = 11100\dots0$, $\text{wt}(S) = 3$, so case I applies.
$S = u_1 + u_2 + u_3$, so $e = 11100\dots0$.

(3.6.2) Decoding Method II (Goethals [67]) This is a clever threshold decoding scheme, using the properties of the designs associated with the code. Since $\mathscr{G}$ is self-dual (3.4.4), any set of codewords can be used as parity checks for the code. Let us see how to decode one coordinate, say the first. Take as parity checks the 253 codewords of weight 8 containing the first coordinate (from Table 3.4.16). If there is exactly one error, the number of parity checks which fail is either 253 or 77, depending on whether or not the first coordinate is in error. If two errors occur, the number of parity check failures is either 176 or $2.56 = 112$ in the two cases. Finally if there are 3 errors, the number of parity check failures is either $120 + 21 = 141$ or $3.40 + 5 = 125$ in the two cases. To summarize:

	First Coordinate	
Number of Errors	in error	not in error
1	253	77
2	176	112
3	141	125

Therefore there is a simple threshold test: if more than 133 out of the 253 parity checks fail, the first coordinate is in error, if less than 133 fail this coordinate is correct.

This test can then be applied successively to all the coordinates (using the fact that the code is invariant under a transitive group).

§ 3.7 Notes and Further Reading

(§ 3.2) For the use of the weight enumerator in obtaining properties of a code, see for example MacWilliams [76], Berlekamp [1] Ch. 16, and Goethals and Snover [68].

(§ 3.4) The code $\mathscr{G}$ was first discovered by Golay [25], [26]. The generator matrix (3.4.1) was found by Paige [77], and later rediscovered by Leech [71] and Karlin [69]. The discussion given here follows Karlin and MacWilliams [70] – see this reference for a proof of Theorem (3.5.4).

Golay gave another perfect code in [25], an [11,6,5] code over the field GF(3). It can be defined by the generator matrix

$$G = \left[\begin{array}{c|c} I_6 & \dfrac{111111}{A} \end{array} \right] ,$$

where A is a circulant with first row $(0,1,-1,-1,1)$ (van Lint [2], p. 103). Perfect codes will be discussed in § 5.10.

In 1967 Leech [72] used the Golay code to construct a very dense sphere packing in 24-dimensional Euclidean space. Conway [63]-[66] has extensively studied the symmetry group of this packing. Many other sphere packings based on codes have been given in [73]-[75]. For example we constructed a nonlattice sphere packing in 10-dimensional space which is denser than what is thought to be the densest lattice packing.

For the proof of Theorem (3.5.2) and the connection between the Golay code and the Mathieu group M_{24}, see Assmus and Mattson [59], Berlekamp [61], and Conway [66].

Several of the properties of Theorem (3.4.2) hold generally for quadratic residue codes — see [1] § 15.2, [2] Ch. 4. For example (3.4.10) is a special case of a theorem of Perron [78].

The connection between codes and designs as illustrated by Theorem (3.4.14) has been studied by Assmus and Mattson [59], [60], Goethals [67], and many others.

Pless [79] has shown that the Golay code is unique.

Tables 3.4.16, 3.4.17 are taken from Conway [66]. Exercise (3.5.16) is from Goethals [67].

(§ 3.6) Berlekamp [62] also considers which error patterns of weight 4 can be corrected.

§3.8 References

[59] Assmus, E.F., Jr., and H.F. Mattson, Jr., (1966), Perfect Codes and The Mathieu Groups, Arch. Math. 17:121-135.

[60] Assmus, E.F., Jr., and H.F. Mattson, Jr., (1969), New 5-Designs, JCT 6:122-151.

[61] Berlekamp, E.R. (1971), Coding Theory and the Mathieu Groups, IC 18:40-64.

[62] Berlekamp, E.R. (1972A), Decoding the Golay Code, JPL Report 32-1526, Vol. IX, pages 81-85.

[63] Conway, J.H. (1968A), A Perfect Group of Order 8,315,553,613,086,720,000 and the Sporadic Simple Groups, Proc. Nat. Acad. Sci. USA, 61:398-400.

[64] Conway, J.H. (1969), A Group of Order 8,315,553,613,086,720,000, Bull. London Math Soc. 1:79-88.

[65] Conway, J.H. (1969A), A Characterization of Leech's Lattice, Inventiones Math. 7:137-142.

[66] Conway, J.H. (1971A), Three Lectures on Exceptional Groups, Pages 215-247 of Finite Simple Groups, Edited by M.B. Powell and G. Highman, Academic Press, N.Y.

[67] Goethals, J.-M. (1971), On the Golay Perfect Binary Code, JCT 11:178-186.

[68] Goethals, J.-M. and S. L. Snover (1972), Nearly Perfect Binary Codes, DM 3:65-88.

[69] Karlin, M. (1969), New Binary Coding Results by Circulants, PGIT 15:81-92.

[70] Karlin, M. and F.J. MacWilliams (197), An Elementary Construction of The Golay Code, to appear.

[71] Leech, J. (1964), Some Sphere Packings in Higher Space, CJM 16:657-682.

[72] Leech, J. (1967), Notes on Sphere Packings, CJM 19:251-267.

[73] Leech, J. and N.J.A. Sloane (1970), New Sphere Packings in Dimensions 9-15, BAMS 76:1006-1010.

[74] Leech, J. and N.J.A. Sloane (1970A), New Sphere Packings in More Than 32 Dimensions, pp. 345-355 of Bose, R.C., et al., Editors (1970), Proc. Second Chapel Hill Conf. on Combinatorial Mathematics and Its Applications, Chapel Hill, N.C.

[75] Leech, J. and N.J.A. Sloane (1971), Sphere Packings and Error-Correcting Codes, CJM 23:718-745.

[76] MacWilliams, F.J. (1963) A Theorem on the Distribution of Weights in a Systematic Code, BSTJ 42:79-94.

[77] Paige, L.J. (1956), A Note on the Mathieu Groups, CJM 9:15-18.

[78] Perron, O. (1952), Bemerkungen Ueber Die Verteilung Der Quadratischen Reste, Math. Zeit. 56:122-130.

[79] Pless, V.S. (1968), On the Uniqueness of the Golay Codes, JCT 5:215-228.

[79a] Sloane, N.J.A., S.M. Reddy and C.-L. Chen (1972), New Binary Codes, PGIT 18:503-510.

§§ 4 The Theorems of MacWilliams and Gleason

§4.1 Introduction

In this chapter we prove two of the most remarkable results in all of coding theory. The first, due to Mrs. F.J. MacWilliams, says that the weigth enumeration of the dual code $\mathcal{C}^{\perp}$ is completely determined just by the weight enumerator of $\mathcal{C}$. The second result, due to A.M. Gleason, states that the weight enumerator of any self-dual code (in which the weigth of any codeword is a multiple of 4) is a polynomial in the weigth enumerators of the extended Hamming code and the extended Golay code. This is an extremely powerful theorem for finding the minimum distance of large self-dual codes. It can also be used to show that certain codes do not exist.

We recall from §3.2 that the **weight enumerator** of a code $\mathcal{C}$ of length n is

(4.1.1)
$$W_{\mathcal{C}}(x,y) = \sum_{u \in \mathcal{C}} x^{n-wt(u)} y^{wt(u)}$$

$$= \sum_{i=0}^{n} A_i x^{n-i} y^i \, ,$$

where A_i is the number of codewords of weight i.

§ 4.2 MacWilliams' Theorem

Let $\mathcal{C}$ be a linear $[n,k]$ code and $\mathcal{C}^{\perp}$ its dual code. Then the weight enumerator $W_{\mathcal{C}^{\perp}}(x,y)$ of $\mathcal{C}^{\perp}$ is uniquely determined by the weight enumerator $W_{\mathcal{C}}(x,y)$ of $\mathcal{C}$:

(4.2.1) **MacWilliams' Theorem**

$$W_{\mathcal{C}^{\perp}}(x,y) = \frac{1}{2^k} W_{\mathcal{C}}(x+y,x-y)$$

The proof is based on the

(4.2.2) **Lemma** Let f: $F^n \to A$ be any mapping into a vector space A over the complex numbers. Define $\hat{f}$: $F^n \to A$ by

$$\hat{f}(u) = \sum_{v \in F^n} f(v)(-1)^{u \cdot v}$$

Then for any linear code $\mathscr{C} \subset F^n$ we have

$$\sum_{v \in \mathscr{C}^\perp} f(v) = \frac{1}{|\mathscr{C}|} \sum_{u \in \mathscr{C}} \hat{f}(u)$$

Proof of lemma:

$$\sum_{u \in \mathscr{C}} \hat{f}(u) = \sum_{u \in \mathscr{C}} \sum_{v \in F^n} f(v)(-1)^{u \cdot v}$$

$$= \sum_{v \in F^n} f(v) \sum_{u \in \mathscr{C}} (-1)^{u \cdot v}$$

If $v \in \mathscr{C}^\perp$, the inner sum is equal to $|\mathscr{C}|$. But if $v \notin \mathscr{C}^\perp$, $u \cdot v = 0$ and 1 equally often and the inner sum is zero. Q.E.D.

Proof of Theorem: Let A be the set of polynomials in x,y with complex coefficients, and $f(v) = x^{n - wt(v)} y^{wt(v)}$. Then

$$\hat{f}(v) = \sum_{v \in F^n} x^{n - wt(v)} y^{wt(v)} (-1)^{u \cdot v}$$

$$= \sum_{v_1 = 0}^{1} \sum_{v_2 = 0}^{1} \sum_{v_n = 0}^{1} \prod_{i = 1}^{n} x^{1 - v_i} y^{v_i} (-1)^{u_i v_i}$$

$$= \prod_{i = 1}^{n} \sum_{v = 0}^{1} x^{1 - v} y^{v} (-1)^{u_i v}$$

If $u_i = 0$, the inner sum is $x + y$; if $u_i = 1$ the inner sum is $x - y$. Therefore,

$$\hat{f}(u) = (x + y)^{n - wt(u)} (x - y)^{wt(u)} \qquad Q.E.D.$$

(4.2.3) **Examples of MacWilliams' Theorem**

$$\mathscr{C} = \underline{0}, \ W_{\mathscr{C}} = x^n; \ \mathscr{C}^\perp = F^n, \ W_{\mathscr{C}^\perp} = (x + y)^n.$$

(4.2.4) $\mathscr{C} = \{\underline{0}, \underline{1}\}$, $W_{\mathscr{C}} = x^n + y^n$; $\mathscr{C}^{\perp} = \{$even weight vectors

of length n$\}$, $W_{\mathscr{C}^{\perp}} = \frac{1}{2}[(x+y)^n + (x-y)^n]$.

(4.2.5) $\mathscr{C} = \{00, 11\} = \mathscr{C}^{\perp}$,

(4.2.6) $W_{\mathscr{C}}(x,y) = x^2 + y^2 = \varphi_1(x,y)$

(4.2.7) For the code (1.1.3), $W_{\mathscr{C}} = x^3 + 3xy^2$,

$W_{\mathscr{C}^{\perp}} = 1/4\left((x+y)^3 + 3(x+y)(x-y)^2\right) = x^3 + y^3$, and $\mathscr{C}^{\perp} = \{000, 111\}$.

(4.2.8) Verify the theorem for (1.1.4) and (1.1.5).

§ 4.3 Gleason's Theorem

When the code is self-dual, (4.2.1) becomes an identity which Gleason (1970) was able to solve:

(4.3.1) **Theorem** (i) Let $\mathscr{C}$ be a binary self-dual code. Then the weight enumerator $W_{\mathscr{C}}$ of $\mathscr{C}$ is a polynomial in the weight enumerators

(4.3.2) $\varphi_1 = x^2 + y^2$

(4.3.3) $\varphi_2 = x^8 + 14x^4 y^4 + y^8$

of the code $\{00,11\}$ and the [8,4,4] extended Hamming code.

Equivalently (replacing φ_2 by $\theta_1 = 1/4(\varphi_1^4 - \varphi_2)$), $W_{\mathscr{C}}$ is a polynomial in φ_1, and

(4.3.4) $\theta_1 = x^2 y^2 (x^2 - y^2)^2$

(ii) Let $\mathscr{C}$ be a binary self-dual code in which the weight of every codeword is a multiple of 4. Then $W_{\mathscr{C}}$ is a polynomial in φ_2 and

(4.3.5) $\varphi_3 = x^{24} + 759x^{16} y^8 + 2576x^{12} y^{12} + 759x^8 y^{16} + y^{24}$,

the weight enumerator (3.4.9) of the extended Golay code.

Equivalently replacing φ_3 by $\theta_2 = 1/42 (\varphi_2^3 - \varphi_3)$, $W_{\mathscr{C}}$ is a polynomial in φ_2 and

$$\theta_2 = x^4 y^4 (x^4 - y^4)^4 \qquad (4.3.6)$$

Proof. The following proof is not the shortest, but (once the necessary background from invariant theory has been developed) it is the simplest, and the easiest proof to generalize to other theorems of the same type.

Let $\mathscr{C}$ be a binary self-dual code with weight enumerator $W(x,y)$.

The MacWilliams theorem (4.2.1) now gives an identity for W:

$$W(x,y) = \frac{1}{2^{n/2}} W(x+y, x-y),$$

or, since W is homogeneous of degree n,

$$W(x,y) = W\left(\frac{x+y}{\sqrt{2}}, \frac{x-y}{\sqrt{2}}\right) \qquad (4.3.7)$$

In other words, $W(x,y)$ is invariant under the linear transformation:

$$\text{replace } \begin{pmatrix} x \\ y \end{pmatrix} \text{ by } T \begin{pmatrix} x \\ y \end{pmatrix}, \qquad (4.3.8)$$

where

$$T = T_1 \overset{\triangle}{=} \frac{1}{\sqrt{2}} \begin{pmatrix} 1 & 1 \\ 1 & -1 \end{pmatrix}. \qquad (4.3.9)$$

Since $\mathscr{C}$ is self-dual, $x \cdot x = 0$ for any $x \in \mathscr{C}$, and therefore $wt(x)$ is even. So (from (4.1.1)) $W(x,y)$ is also invariant under the transformation (4.3.8) when

$$T = T_2 \overset{\triangle}{=} \begin{pmatrix} 1 & 0 \\ 0 & -1 \end{pmatrix}. \qquad (4.3.10)$$

Therefore W is invariant under the group generated by T_1 and T_2. This is a group G_1 (say), of order 16, isomorphic to the dihedral group of order 16.

In case (ii), we may replace T_2 by

$$T_3 \overset{\triangle}{=} \begin{pmatrix} 1 & 0 \\ 0 & i \end{pmatrix}, \qquad (4.3.11)$$

and T_1, T_3 generate a group G_2 (say) of order 192.

Thus to prove the theorem it will be sufficient to specify which polynomials are invariant under the groups G_1 and G_2.

§ 4.4 Invariant Theory

The problems stated at the end of the previous section are special cases of the general problem of finding the invariant polynomials of a group of linear transformations. The classical statement and solution of this problem are as follows (see [81, Ch. 17], [87, Part II], [89]):

(4.4.1) **The Problem** Let G be a finite group of linear trnsformations on n (complex) variables $x_1, x_2, ... x_n$; that is, G is a multiplicative group of nonsingular complex n x n matrices. Let g be the order of G, and let I denote the identity matrix.

A typical element $A = (a_{ij})$ of G thus stands for the linear transformation:

$$(4.4.2) \qquad \texttt{replace } x_i \texttt{ by } \sum_{j=1}^{n} a_{ij} x_j \texttt{ , for } i = 1,2,...,n.$$

We use the same symbol A both for a transformation and for the matrix describing it.

If $f(\underline{x}) = f(x_1, ..., x_n)$ is any polynomial, let $Af(\underline{x}) = f(A\underline{x})$ denote the polynomial obtained by applying the transformation (4.4.2) to the variables $x_1, ..., x_n$.

Def. $f(\underline{x})$ is an **invariant** polynomial of G if

$$Af(\underline{x}) = f(\underline{x}), \texttt{ for all } A \in G.$$

Clearly if f, g are invariants so are f+g and fg; therefore the invariants of G form a ring $\mathscr{P}(G)$.

The main problem is to characterize $\mathscr{P}(G)$. It is sufficient to characterize the invariants which are homogeneous polynomials, since any invariant is a sum of homogeneous invariants.

(4.4.2) Existence of a Basic Set of Invariants for Finite Groups

Def. Polynomials $f_1(\underline{x}), ..., f_m(\underline{x})$ are **algebraically dependent** if there is a polynomial p with complex coefficients, not all zero, such that $p(f_1(\underline{x}), ..., f_m(\underline{x})) \equiv 0$. Otherwise $f_1(\underline{x}), ..., f_m(\underline{x})$ are **algebraically independent**

(4.4.3) **Theorem** ([83, p. 154]) Any n +1 polynomials in n varibles are algebraically dependent.

(4.4.4) **Theorem** ([81, p. 357]) There exist n algebraically independent invariants

$f_1,...,f_n$ in $\mathscr{P}(G)$; and so (by Th. 4.4.3) any invariant is a root of a polynomial equation in $f_1,...,f_n$.

(4.4.5) **Theorem** ([81 p. 359]) There always exist $n+1$ invariants $f_1,...,f_{n+1}$ in $\mathscr{P}(G)$ such that any invariant is a rational function in $f_1,...,f_{n+1}$.

However, by far the most convenient description of $\mathscr{P}(G)$ is a set of invariants $f_1,...,f_m$ such that any invariant is a **polynomial** in $f_1,...,f_m$. Then $f_1,...,f_m$ is called a **polynomial basis** for $\mathscr{P}(G)$. By Th. 4.4.3 if $m > n$ there will be polynomial equations, which are called **syzygies**, relating $f_1,...,f_m$.

(4.4.6) **Noether's Theorem** ([88, pp. 275-6]) $\mathscr{P}(G)$ has a polynomial basis consisting of not more than $\binom{g+n}{n}$ invariants, of degree not exceeding g.

Theorem 4.4.6 says that a polynomial basis for $\mathscr{P}(G)$ can always be found. Finding invariants is fairly easy using:

(4.4.7) **Theorem** If $f(\underline{x})$ is any polynomial then

$$h(\underline{x}) = \frac{1}{g} \sum_{A \in G} Af(\underline{x}) \qquad (4.4.8)$$

is an invariant of G.

Proof. For any $A' \in G$.

$$h(A'\underline{x}) = \frac{1}{g} \sum_{A \in G} f(A'A\underline{x}) = \frac{1}{g} \sum_{A \in G} f(A\underline{x}) = h(x)$$

since the last sum is a rearrangement of the one before.

Q.E.D.

Furthermore, it is clear that all invariants of G can be obtained in this way. In fact the proof of Theorem 4.4.6 shows that a polynomial basis for the invariants of G can be obtained by averaging over G all monomials.

$$x_1^{b_1} x_2^{b_2} ... x_n^{b_n}$$

of total degree $\Sigma b_i \leqslant g$.

More generally, any symmetric function of the g polynomials $\{f(A\underline{x}); A \in G\}$ is an invariant of G.

Finally, Theorems 4.4.9, 4.4.10 enable one to determine when enough invariants have been found to make a basis.

(4.4.9) **Theorem** ([87, p. 258]) The number of linearly independent invariants of G of the first degree is

$$\frac{1}{g} \sum_{A \in G} \text{trace } (A) .$$

(4.4.10) **Theorem** (Molien, [88], [87, p. 259]) The number of linearly independent invariants of G of degree ν is the coefficient of λ^{ν} in the expansion of

$$(4.4.11) \qquad\qquad \Phi(\lambda) = \frac{1}{g} \sum_{A \in G} \frac{1}{\det| I - \lambda A |}$$

We call $\Phi(\lambda)$ the **Molien series** of G.

(4.4.12) **A Simple Example** We shall make an exception here and consider a code $\mathscr{C}$ over GF(q). The Hamming weight wt(u) of a vector u is still the number of its nonzero components. Also the weight enumerator is still defined as

$$W_{\mathscr{C}}(x,y) = \sum_{u \in \mathscr{C}} x^{n - wt(u)}\, y^{wt(u)}.$$

The MacWilliams theorem now says that

$$(4.4.13) \qquad\qquad W_{\mathscr{C}}\perp(x,y) = \frac{1}{|\mathscr{C}|}\, W_{\mathscr{C}}(x + (q-1)y, x - y)$$

(which reduces to (4.2.1) when q = 2). If $\mathscr{C}$ is a self-dual code (4.4.13) implies that $W_{\mathscr{C}}$ is invariant under the transformation

$$T_4 = \frac{1}{\sqrt{q}}\, \begin{pmatrix} 1 & q-1 \\ 1 & -1 \end{pmatrix}$$

The group G_4 generated by T_4 is of order 2: $G_4 = \{ I, T_4 \}$, since $T_4^2 = I$.

Let us find the invariants of G_4.

Using (4.4.7) with $f(\underline{x}) = x$ we obtain the invariant $x + 1/\sqrt{q}$ $(x + (q-1)y)$, or equivalently $\varphi_1 = x + (\sqrt{q} - 1)\, y$. Using (4.4.7) with $f(\underline{x}) = x^2$ we obtain the invariant $x^2 + 1/q(x + (q-1)y)^2$, or equivalently, subtracting $(1 + 1/q)\varphi_1^2$, $\varphi_2 = y(x - y)$.

Any polynomial in φ_1, φ_2 is of course an invariant of G_4, and the number of products $\varphi_1^i \varphi_2^j$ of degree ν is equal to the number of solutions of $i + 2j = \nu$, which is the coefficient of λ^{ν} in

$$(4.4.14)\quad (1 + \lambda + \lambda^2 + ...)(1 + \lambda^2 + \lambda^4 + ...) = 1/\{(1 - \lambda)(1 - \lambda^2)\}\ .$$

To see if this includes all the invariants of G we compute the Molien series (4.4.11). This is

$$\Phi(\lambda) = \frac{1}{2} \left(\frac{1}{(1-\lambda)^2} + \frac{1}{1-\lambda^2} \right) = \frac{1}{(1-\lambda)(1-\lambda^2)}$$

which agrees with (4.4.14)! We conclude that we have found all the invariants, i.e., that Φ_1, Φ_2 are a polynomial basis for the invariants of G.

For coding applications we are interested in invariants of even degree. This corresponds to extending the group by adding the matrix -I, and the Molien series becomes

$$\Phi_e(\lambda) = \frac{1}{2} \left(\Phi(\lambda) + \Phi(-\lambda) \right) = \frac{1}{(1-\lambda^2)^2} \quad,$$

and as a basis we may take φ_1^2, φ_2, or equivalently $\varphi_3 = x^2 + (q-1)xy, \varphi_4 = xy - y^2$. Thus we have shown that the Hamming weight enumerator of any self-dual code over GF(q) is a polynomial in φ_3 and φ_4.

For example, the code generated by {11} (which is self-dual if q is even) has weight enumerator $\varphi_3 - (q-1)\varphi_4$.

The preceding argument enables us to give a short proof of a recent result of Leontjev.

(4.4.15) **Theorem** (Leontjev (1973))

For a linear code $\mathscr{C}$ over GF(q),

$$W_{\mathscr{C}}(x,y) W_{\mathscr{C}} \left(\frac{x + (q-1)y}{\sqrt{q}} \,, \, \frac{x-y}{\sqrt{q}} \right)$$

is a polynomial in $x^2 + (q-1)xy$ and $xy-y^2$.

Proof. This product is clearly invariant under T_4 and -I.

§ 4.5 Concluding the Proof of Gleason's Theorem

The proof is now very easy, using the machinery of the previous section. It is straigthforward to compute the Molien series for G_1 and G_2 :

$$\Phi_{G_1}(\lambda) = \frac{1}{(1-\lambda^2)(1-\lambda^8)} \quad, \qquad\qquad (4.5.1)$$

$$(4.5.2) \qquad\qquad \Phi_{G_2}(\lambda) = \frac{1}{(1 - \lambda^8)(1 - \lambda^{24})} \ .$$

Now φ_1 and θ_1 are algebraically independent invariants of G_1, of degrees 2 and 8, and the number of products $\varphi_1^i \theta_1^j$ of degree v is equal to the coefficient of λ^v in (4.5.1). Therefore φ_1 and θ_1 are a polynomial basis for the invariants of G_1, which proves the first part of the theorem. The second part follows in the same way from (4.5.2).

Q.E.D.

§ 4.6 Applications of Gleason's Theorem

(4.6.1) **Example 1** A self-dual code of length 12 contains no codewords of weight 2. What is its weight enumerator W? By Th. (4.3.1) (i) W has the form

$$W = a_1 \varphi_1^6 + a_2 \varphi_1^2 \theta_1$$

$$= a_1 (x^{12} + 6x^{10} y^2 + ...)$$

$$+ a_2 (x^4 + 2x^2 y^2 + y^4) x^2 y^2 (x^2 - y^2)^2$$

But since there are no words of weigth 2, this is also

$$= x^{12} + 0.x^{10} y^2 + ...$$

Therefore $a_1 = 1$, $a_2 = -6$, and

$$W = x^{12} + 15x^8 y^4 + 32x^6 y^6 + 15x^4 y^8 + y^{12}$$

Aside: a generator matrix for this code is

$$\begin{pmatrix} 1 & 1 & 1 & 1 & & & & & & & & \\ & & 1 & 1 & 1 & 1 & & & & & & \\ & & & & 1 & 1 & 1 & 1 & & & & \\ & & & & & & 1 & 1 & 1 & 1 & & \\ & & & & & & & & 1 & 1 & 1 & 1 \\ 1 & & & 1 & & & 1 & & & 1 & & 1 \end{pmatrix}$$

(4.6.2) **Example 2** Is there a self-dual code of length 32 with minimum distance 10? By Th. (4.3.1) (i), its weight enumerator W has the form

$$W = a_1\varphi_1^{16} + a_2\varphi_1^{12}\theta_1 + a_3\varphi_1^8\theta_1^2 + a_4\varphi_1^4\theta_1^3 + a_5\theta_1^4$$

$$= x^{32} + 0x^{30}y^2 + 0x^{28}y^4 + 0x^{26}y^6 + 0x^{24}y^8 + A_{10} + x^{22}y^{10} + ...$$

Equating coefficients we find that $a_1,...,a_5$ are uniquely determined and that

$$W = x^{32} + 4960x^{22}y^{10} - 3472x^{20}y^{12} + ...$$

Since a weight enumerator cannot have a negative coefficient, no such code exists.

(4.6.3) **Exercise** Take all the codewords in the [24,12,8] extended Golay code which begins either with 00... or 11..., and delete the first two coordinates. Use Gleason's theorem to obtain the weight distribution of the code.

(Answer: $x^{22} + y^{22} + 77(x^{16}y^6 + x^6y^{16}) + 330(x^{14}y^8 + x^8y^{14}) + 616(x^{12}y^{10} + x^{10}y^{12}))$.

(4.6.4) **Example 3** Let $\mathscr{C}$ be a self-dual code of length $n = 8j$ in which all weights are divisible by 4. What is its greatest possible minimum distance? By Th. (4.3.1) (ii), with $m = [n/24]$,

$$W = \sum_{k=0}^{m} a_k\varphi_2^{j-3k}\theta_2^k \,,$$

which contains $m + 1$ parameters a_k. With the correct choice of these parameters, we can make W take the form

$$W = x^n + A_{4m+4}y^{4m+4}x^{n-(4m+4)} + ... , \qquad (4.6.5)$$

which corresponds to a hypothetical code with minimum distance at least $4m+4$. Of course if it should turn out that $A_{4m+4} = 0$, the minimum distance would be greater than $4m+4$. However, Mallows and Sloane [85a] showed that

$$A_{4m+4} = \begin{cases} \binom{n}{5}\binom{5m-2}{m-1}\Big/\binom{4m+4}{5}, & \text{if } n = 24m; \\[2ex] \dfrac{1}{4}\, n(n-1)(n-2)(n-4)\, \dfrac{(5m)!}{m!\,(4m+4)!}, & \text{if } n = 24m+8; \\[2ex] \dfrac{3}{2}\, n(n-2)\, \dfrac{(5m+2)!}{m!\,(4m+4)!}, & \text{if } n = 24m+16; \end{cases}$$

and thus proved:

(4.6.6) **Theorem** The minimum distance of a self-dual code (with weights divisible by 4) is at most $4\,[n/24]+4$.

(This improves on the Elias bound, which for large n is $d/n \leqslant 0.196$ at rate $1/2$)

(4.6.5) is called an **extremal** weight enumerator. It is not known in general if a code exists with this weight enumerator (*). When n is a multiple of 24 such extremal codes, if they exist, are of particular interest since by the theorem of Assmus and Mattson quoted in §3.4 the codewords of any fixed weight form 5-designs. The exremal codes of lengths 24 and 48 do exist: they are the Golay code and a quadratic residue code. The next case is an

(4.6.7) **Unsolved Problem** Is there a self-dual [72,36] code with the following weight distribution?

(*) Recent work of Mrs. F.J. MacWilliams has shown that for all n sufficiently large such codes do not exist.

weight i		A_i
1	72	1
16	56	249849
20	52	18106704
24	48	462962955
28	44	4397342400
32	40	16602715899
	36	25756721120

§4.7 Notes and Further Reading

(§4.2) MacWilliams' theorem first appeared in [84] and [76]; the proof given here follows Van Lint [2]. Numerous generalizations of this theorem to offer kinds of weight enumerators have been given by MacWIlliams [84], MacWilliams, Sloane and Goethals [52] and MacWilliams, Mallows and Sloane [85]. All these generalizations ultimately depend on Lemma (4.2.2).

(§4.3) Gleason's theorem appeared in [82]. A number of proofs were given by Berlekamp, MacWilliams, and Sloane [80], and the invariant theory proof given here may be found, along with a number of generalizations of the theorem, in MacWilliams, Mallows, and Sloane [85].

Gleasons's paper also gave a version of his theorem which applies to self-dual codes over GF(3), and then applied this to show that a code of length 72 and minimum distance 21 cannot exist, by showing that the weight enumerator must contain a negative coefficient. Mallows and Sloane [85a] generalized this by showing that for all sufficiently large n the best ternary weight eneumerator contains a negative coefficient.

The examples (4.4.12), (4.5.1) and (4.5.2) show how convenient it is when the Molien series can be put into the form

$$\frac{\sum_{j=0}^{r} a_j \lambda^{b_j}}{\prod_{i=1}^{n} \left(1 - \lambda^{d_i}\right)},$$

where a_j, b_j and d_i are positive integers. It turns out that the Molien series for a finite group can always be put into this form. See Mallows and Sloane [86] for further details.

§ 4.8 References

[80] Berlekamp, E.R., F.J. MacWilliams and N.J.A. Sloane (1972), Gleason's Theorem on Self-Dual Codes, PGIT 18:409-414.

[81] Burnside, W. (1911), Theory of Groups of Finite Order, Second ed., Reprinted by Dover, N.Y. 1955.

[82] Gleason, A.M. (1970), Weight Polynomials of Self-Dual Codes and the MacWilliams Identities, Actes, Congr. Inter. Math., Nice 1970, Gauthier-Villars, Paris, Vol. 3:211-215.

[83] Jacobson, N. (1964), Lectures in Abstract Algebra, Vol. 3, Van Nostrand, Princeton, N.J.

[83a] Leontjev, V.K. (1973), Spectra of Linear Codes, Third International Symposium on Information Theory, Tallinn, Estonia, June 1973, Abstracts of Papers, Part II, pp. 102-106.

[84] MacWilliams, F.J. (1962), Combinatorial Problems of Elementary Abelian Groups, Ph.D. Thesis, Dept. of Math., Harvard University, May, 1962.

[85] MacWIlliams, F.J., C.L. Mallows, and N.J.A. Sloane (1972), Generalizations of Gleason's Theorem on Weight Enumerators of Self-Dual Codes, PGIT 18:794-805.

[85a] Mallows, C.L. and N.J.A. Sloane (1973), An Upper Bound for Self-Dual Codes, IC 22: 188-200.

[86] Mallows, C.L. and N.J.A. Sloane (197), On the Invariants of a Linear Group of Order 336, Proc. Camb. Phil. Soc., To Appear.

[87] Müller, G.A., H.F. Blichfeldt, and L.E. Dickson (1916), Theory and Applications of Finite Groups, Reprinted by Dover, N.Y. 1961.

[88]   Molien, T. (1897), Ueber die Invarianten der Linear Substitutionsgruppen, Sitzungsber. Koenig. Preuss. Akad. Wiss., pp. 1152-1156.

[89]   Weyl, H. (1946), The Classical Groups, Princeton University Press, Princeton, N.J.

§ § 5 Cyclic Codes

§ 5.1 Introduction

Cyclic codes are the most studied of all codes. After giving some of the general theory in the first few sections, we proceed with a brief description of the Hamming, BCH, Reed-Solomon, and Justesen codes, with a digression on perfect codes.

§ 5.2 Definition of Cyclic Code

(5.2.1) **Definition** A code $\mathscr{C}$ is **cyclic** if it is linear and if any cyclic shift of a codeword is also a codeword. I.e., if $(a_0, a_1, ..., a_{n-1}) \in \mathscr{C}$ then $(a_{n-1}, a_0, a_1, ..., a_{n-2}) \in \mathscr{C}$. For example (1.1.2)-(1.1.5) are cyclic codes.

To get an algebraic description, we associate with the vector $a = (a_0, a_1, ..., a_{n-1})$ in F^n the polynomial $a(x) = a_0 + a_1 x + ... + a_{n-1} x^{n-1}$. (Think of $a(x)$ as a generating function for a.) $a(x)$ is an element of $\mathscr{R}_n = F[x]/(x^n + 1)$; i.e., of the ring of polynomials modulo $x^n + 1$.

If we multiply $a(x)$ by x we get

$$xa(x) = a_0 x + a_1 x^2 + ... + a_{n-2} x^{n-1} + a_{n-1} x^n$$
$$= a_{n-1} + a_0 x + ... + a_{n-2} x^{n-1}$$

(in $\mathscr{R}_n$) which is associated with the vector $(a_{n-1}, a_0, ..., a_{n-2})$. Thus multiplying by x in $\mathscr{R}_n$ corresponds to a cyclic shift of the vector.

(5.2.2) **Definition** An **ideal** $\mathscr{G}$ of $\mathscr{R}_n$ is a linear subspace of $\mathscr{R}_n$ such that if $a(x) \in \mathscr{G}$ then $xa(x) \in \mathscr{G}$.

Therefore if $a(x) \in \mathscr{G}$ then $r(x)a(x) \in \mathscr{G}$ for any $r(x) \in \mathscr{R}_n$.

It is clear from the above discussion that we can rephrase our definition as

(5.2.3) **Definition** A **cyclic code** of length n is an ideal in $\mathscr{R}_n$.

§5.3 Generator Polynomial

(5.3.1) **Definition** A **principal ideal** $\mathcal{G}$ in $\mathcal{R}_n$ consists of all multiples of a fixed polynomial $g(x)$:

$$\mathcal{G} = \{\, r(x)\,g(x) \mid r(x) \in \mathcal{R}_n \,\},$$

$$= \,< g(x)>\ .$$

$g(x)$ is called the **generator** polynomial of the ideal.

In fact every ideal in $\mathcal{R}_n$ is a principal ideal; every cyclic code has a generator polynomial.

(5.3.2) **Theorem** Let $\mathcal{G}$ be a nonzero ideal in $\mathcal{R}_n$, i.e., a cyclic code of length n.

(a) There is a unique polynomial $g(x)$ of minimal degree in $\mathcal{G}$.

(b) $\mathcal{G} = <g(x)>$, i.e., $g(x)$ is the generator polynomial of $\mathcal{G}$.

(c) $g(x)$ is a factor of $x^n + 1$.

(d) Let $r = \deg g(x)$. Then the dimension of $\mathcal{G}$ is n-r, and any $a(x) \in \mathcal{G}$ has a unique representation as $a(x) = b(x)g(x)$, $\deg b(x) < $ n-r.

(e) If $g(x) = g_0 + g_1 x + \dots + g_r x^r$ then $\mathcal{G}$ is generated (as a subspace of F^n) by the rows of the generator matrix

$$G = \begin{bmatrix} g_0 & g_1 & g_2 & \cdots & g_r & & & 0 \\ & g_0 & g_1 & \cdots & g_{r-1} & g_r & & \\ & & & \cdots & & & & \\ 0 & & & g_0 & \cdots & & & g_r \end{bmatrix}$$

Proof. (a) Suppose $f(x), g(x) \in \mathcal{G}$ both have the minimal degree r. But then $f(x) + g(x) \in \mathcal{G}$ has lower degree, a contradiction unless $f(x) = g(x)$. (b) Suppose $a(x) \in \mathcal{G}$. Write $a(x) = b(x)g(x) + r(x)$, where $\deg r(x) < r$. But $r(x) \in \mathcal{G}$ so $r(x) = 0$. Therefore $a(x) \in <g(x)>$. (c) Write $x^n + 1 = b(x)g(x) + r(x)$, where $\deg r(x) < r$. In $\mathcal{R}_n$ this says $r(x) = b(x)g(x) \in \mathcal{G}$, a contradiction unless $r(x) = 0$. (d), (e): Clearly $g(x), xg(x), \dots, x^{n-r-1}g(x)$ are linearly independent elements of $\mathcal{G}$. The corresponding vectors are the rows of G. Thus there are 2^{n-r} distinct vectors in $\mathcal{G}$ of the form $b(x)g(x)$, $\deg b(x) < $ n-r. Furthermore, any element $c(x)g(x)$ is equal to such a

$b(x)g(x)$ modulo $x^n + 1$, and so these are all the elements of $\mathcal{G}$.

§ 5.4 Check Polynomial

Let $\mathcal{G}$ be a cyclic code with generator polynomial $g(x)$. Then

$$h(x) = (x^n + 1)/g(x) = \sum_{i=0}^{k} h_i x^i \qquad (5.4.1)$$

is called the **check polynomial** of $\mathcal{G}$. In fact, if $c(x) = \sum_{i=0}^{n-1} c_i x^i = a(x)g(x)$ is any codeword of $\mathcal{G}$, then

$$c(x)h(x) = \sum_{i=0}^{n-1} c_i x^i \sum_{j=0}^{k} h_j x^j \qquad (5.4.2)$$

$$= a(x)g(x)h(x) = 0 \quad \text{in } \mathcal{R}_n .$$

The coefficient of x^j in this product is

$$\sum_{i=0}^{n-1} c_i h_{j-i} = 0, \quad j = 0,1,\ldots,n-1 \qquad (5.4.3)$$

where the subscripts are taken modulo n. (5.4.3) are the parity check equations satisfied by the code. Let H denote the n x n parity check matrix

$$H = \begin{bmatrix} & & & h_k & \cdots & h_2 & & h_1 & & h_0 \\ & & h_k & \cdots & h_2 & h_1 & & h_0 & & \\ & & & \cdots\cdots\cdots\cdots & & & & & \\ h_k & \cdots & h_2 & h_1 & h_0 & & & & \end{bmatrix} \qquad (5.4.4)$$

Then $\underline{c} = (c_0, c_1, \ldots, c_{n-1}) \in \mathcal{G}$ if and only if $\underline{c}H = 0$.

Note that

$$k = \deg h(x) = n - \deg g(x) = \text{dimension } \mathcal{G} \qquad (5.4.5)$$

§ 5.5 The Dual Code

Let $\mathcal{G}$ be a cyclic code with generator polynomial $g(x)$ and check polynomial $h(x) = (x^n + 1)/g(x)$.

(5.5.1) **Theorem** The dual code $\mathscr{G}^\perp$ is cyclic and has generator polynomial

$$g^\perp(x) = x^{\deg h(x)} h(x^{-1})$$

Proof. From Eq. (5.4.4),   Q.E.D.

§ 5.6 The Factors of $x^n + 1$

From now on we suppose that n is odd. Let m be the smallest integer such that n divides $2^m - 1$. m is called the **multiplicative order of 2 modulo n.** Then $x^n + 1$ divides $x^{2^m 1} + 1$. Furthermore the zeros of $x^n + 1$, which are called nth roots of unity, lie in the extension field $GF(2^m)$, and in no smaller field. $GF(2^m)$ is therefore called the **splitting field** of $x^n + 1$. We factor $x^n + 1$ in two ways, over $GF(2^m)$ and over $GF(2)$.

(i) There are n distinct elements $\alpha_0, \alpha_1, ..., \alpha_{n-1}$ in $GF(2^m)$ such that

(5.6.1) $$x^n + 1 = \prod_{i=0}^{n-1} (x + \alpha_i).$$

Furthermore, the zeros of $x^n + 1$ form a cyclic subgroup of the nonzero elements of $GF(2^m)$. I.e., there is an element α in $GF(2^m)$, called a primitive nth root of unity, such that

(5.6.2) $$x^n + 1 = \prod_{i=0}^{n-1} (x + \alpha^i).$$

(ii) Divide the integers modulo n into **Cyclotomic classes** of the form

(5.6.3) $$C_s = \{s, 2s, 2^2 s, ..., 2^{m_s - 1} s\},$$

where $s2^{m_s} \equiv s$, modulo n. For example, n = 15:

$$C_0 = 0,$$
$$C_1 = 1, 2, 4, 8,$$
$$C_3 = 3, 6, 12, 9,$$
$$C_5 = 5, 10,$$
$$C_7 = 7, 14, 13, 11.$$

The subscript s is the smallest integer in the class C_s. The set of subscripts are called the class representatives modulo n. Then

$$M^{(s)}(x) = \prod_{i \in C_s} (x - \alpha^i) \tag{5.6.4}$$

has coefficients from GF(2). Also

$$x^n + 1 = \prod_s M^{(s)}(x) \tag{5.6.5}$$

where s runs through the set of class representatives. This is the factorization of $x^n + 1$ into irreducible polynomials over GF(2). $M^{(s)}(x)$ is the lowest degree polynomial having α^s as a zero, and is called the **minimal polynomial of** α^s. Example

$$x^{15} + 1 = M^{(0)}(x) \quad M^{(1)}(x) \quad M^{(3)}(x) \quad M^{(5)}(x) \quad M^{(7)}(x),$$

$$M^{(0)}(x) = x + 1,$$
$$M^{(1)}(x) = x^4 + x + 1,$$
$$M^{(3)}(x) = x^4 + x^3 + x^2 + x + 1,$$
$$M^{(5)}(x) = x^2 + x + 1,$$
$$M^{(7)}(x) = x^4 + x^3 + 1.$$

An important special case of (5.6.5) occurs when $n = 2^m - 1$. Then we have

$$x^{2^m} + x = \text{product of all distinct irreducible polynomials over GF(2) whose degree}$$
divides m.
$$\tag{5.6.6}$$

Example

$$x^2 + x = x(x + 1)$$
$$x^4 + x = x(x + 1)(x^2 + x + 1)$$
$$x^8 + x = x(x + 1)(x^3 + x + 1)(x^3 + x^2 + 1).$$

Exercises

(5.6.7) Find the irreducible factors of x^n+1 for $n \leqslant 16$.

(5.6.8) Show that if s is relatively prime to n, then C_s contains m elements.

(5.6.9) Let $f(x) = \prod_{i \in K} (x + \alpha^i)$, where K is a subset of $\{0,1,...,n-1\}$. Show that $f(x)$ has coefficients which are 0 and 1 if and only if $k \in K \Rightarrow 2k \in K$ modulo n.

(5.6.10) **The basic inversion formula** The vector $\underline{a} = (a_0, a_1, ..., a_{n-1})$ may be recovered from the associated polynomial $a(x) = a_0 + a_1 x + ... + a_{n-1} x^{n-1}$ by

$$a_i = \sum_{j=0}^{n-1} a(\alpha^j) \alpha^{-ij}.$$

§ 5.7 The BCH Bound

This is a very useful lower bound on the minimum distance of a cyclic code.

As usual α denotes a primitive n-th root of unity.

(5.7.1) **Theorem** (The "BCH bound".) Let $\mathscr{C}$ be a cyclic code of length n with generator polynomial

$$g(x) = \prod_{i \in k} (x - \alpha^i)$$

where $K \subset \{0,1,...,n-1\}$. Suppose K contains a string of d_0-1 consecutive integers $b, b+1, ..., b+d_0-2$. Then the minimum distance of $\mathscr{C}$ is at least d_0.

Proof. For any codeword $c(x) \in \mathscr{C}$ we have $c(\alpha^i) = 0$, $\forall i \in K$. Therefore the parity check matrix contains the submatrix H', where

(5.7.2)
$$H' = \begin{bmatrix} 1 & \alpha^b & \alpha^{2b} & \cdots & \alpha^{(n-1)\cdot b} \\ 1 & \alpha^{b+1} & \alpha^{2(b+1)} & \cdots & \alpha^{(n-1)(b+1)} \\ & \cdots & & & \cdots \\ 1 & \alpha^{b+d_0-2} & \alpha^{2(b+d_0-2)} & \cdots & \alpha^{(n-1)(b+d_0-2)} \end{bmatrix}$$

Consider the determinant of any set of $u = d_0 - 1$ distinct columns of H':

$$\det \begin{bmatrix} \alpha^{i_1 b} & \cdots & \alpha^{i_u b} \\ \alpha^{i_1(b+1)} & \cdots & \alpha^{i_u(b+1)} \\ \cdots & \cdots & \cdots \\ \alpha^{i_1(b+d_0-2)} & \cdots & \alpha^{i_u(b+d_0-2)} \end{bmatrix}$$

$$= \alpha^{b(i_1 + \cdots + i_u)} \prod_{1 \leqslant r < s \leqslant u} (\alpha^{i_r} - \alpha^{i_s}) \neq 0,$$

since this is a Vandermonde determinant. Therefore no codeword in the null space of H' has weight $\leqslant d_0 - 1$.   Q.E.D.

§ 5.8 Hamming Codes

The Hamming single-error-correcting codes are probably the most famous of all codes.

(5.8.1) **Definition** The **Hamming code** of length $n = 2^m - 1$ is the cyclic code with generator polynomial $g(x) = M^{(1)}(x) = $ minimal polynomial of α.

Thus the parity check matrix is

$$H = [1, \alpha, \alpha^2, \alpha^3, \dots, \alpha^{n-1}],$$ (5.8.2)

where each α^i is to be expanded as a binary column vector of length m. Since α is a primitive n-th root of unity, all these columns are distinct. Thus they comprise all the distinct nonzero binary vectors of length m.

E.g., when $m = 3$, $b = 7$, and α is a root of $x^3 + x + 1$:

$$H = \begin{bmatrix} 0 & 0 & 1 & 0 & 1 & 1 & 1 \\ 0 & 1 & 0 & 1 & 1 & 1 & 0 \\ 1 & 0 & 0 & 1 & 0 & 1 & 1 \end{bmatrix}$$ (5.8.3)

Apart from the order of columns, this is the H matrix for the code (1.1.5) given in (2.2.3).

(5.8.4) **Theorem** The Hamming code is a

$$[n = 2^m - 1, \quad k = n - m, \quad d = 3]$$

code, with $r = m$ parity checks.

First proof. From Theorem 5.7.1, since α and α^2 are roots of g(x).

Second proof. From Theorem 2.4.7, a code can correct single errors (i.e., has d =3), if and only if the columns of its H matrix are distinct and nonzero.   Q.E.D.

The first few Hamming codes have the parameters [3,1,3]; [7,4,3] (displayed in (1.1.5)), [15,11,3], [31,26,3],... .

(5.8.5) **Decoding** a Hamming code is particularly easy. Suppose we take the columns of H as binary vectors in increasing numerical order, as illustrated by

(5.8.6)
$$
H = \begin{matrix} & 1 & 2 & 3 & 4 & 5 & 6 & 7 \\ & \begin{bmatrix} 0 & 0 & 0 & 1 & 1 & 1 & 1 \\ 0 & 1 & 1 & 0 & 0 & 1 & 1 \\ 1 & 0 & 1 & 0 & 1 & 0 & 1 \end{bmatrix} \end{matrix}
$$

If a single error occurs in coordinate i, then by (2.4.7) the syndrome is the binary representation of i!

§ 5.9 Simplex Codes

(5.9.1) **Definition** The **simplex code** of length n is the dual of the Hamming code of the same length.

Thus the generator matrix of the simplex code is the H matrix of the Hamming code, and the check polynomial is $h(x) = M^{(1)}(x)$. Example: (1.1.4) is a simplex code.

(5.9.2) **Theorem** The simplex code is a

$$[n = 2^m - 1, \quad k = m, \quad d = 2^{m-1}]$$

code, and consists of $\underline{0}$ and the 2^m-1 cyclic shifts of the generator polynomial $g(x) = (x^n+1)/h(x)$.

Proof. Suppose two cyclic shifts $x^i g(x)$, $x^j g(x)$ (i <j) were equal modulo x^n+1. Therefore h(x) divides $x^{i-j}+1$. But this is impossible, for n is the smallest integer for which $h(x) = M^{(1)}(x)$ divides x^n+1. Then (5.8.6) plainly shows that the weight of any nonzero codeword is 2^{m-1}.

(5.9.3) **Remark** The distance between any two codewords is a constant, 2^{m-1}, so the codewords lie at the vertices of a simplex inscribed in the n-dimensional unit cube.

The weight enumerator of the simplex code is

$$x^n + nx^{(n-1)/2} y^{(n+1)/2} \qquad\qquad (5.9.4)$$

(5.9.5) **Exercise** Use the MacWilliams Theorem and (5.9.4) to obtain the weight enumerator of the Hamming code.

If we add an overall parity check to a simplex code, and take the union of the resulting code and its complement, we get a $[\, 2^m, m+1, 2^{m-1}\,]$ Hadamard code (c.f. 1.1.7). (Or alternatively, if we add an overall parity check to a simplex code, and replace 0 by + 1, 1 by -1, the resulting array of codewords forms a Hadamard matrix).

§ 5.10 Perfect Codes

They are $\binom{n}{r}$ binary vectors at a distance r from a given vector $\underline{x}$ of of length n. The

$$\binom{n}{0} + \binom{n}{1} + \ldots + \binom{n}{t}$$

vectors at distance $\leqslant t$ from $\underline{x}$ form a sphere (in the Hamming metric) of radius t.

If $\mathscr{C}$ is an $(n, M, d = 2t+1)$ t-error-connecting code, these spheres of radius t about each codeword must be distinct. The total number of vectors in all these spheres must not exceed 2^n, so:

$$M \left(\binom{n}{0} + \binom{n}{1} + \ldots + \binom{n}{t} \right) \leqslant 2^n \qquad\qquad (5.10.1)$$

This is known as the **Hamming** or **sphere-packing bound**.

(5.10.2) **Definition** A code for which equality holds in (5.10.1) is called **perfect**, or **close-packed**.

Exercise What is the distribution $\{\alpha_i\}$ of the coset representatives, and the probability of correct decoding (2.4.2) for a perfect code?

Example The trivial $[\,n\ \text{odd}, 1, n\,]$ and $[\,n = 2^m, m, 1\,]$ codes are perfect.

(5.10.3) **Theorem** The Hamming $[\,n = 2^m - 1,\ k = n-m,\ d = 3\,]$ and Golay $[\,23, 12, 7\,]$ codes are perfect.

Proof. By verification that (5.10.1) holds:

$$2^{n-m}(1 + 2^m - 1) = 2^n$$

$$2^{12} \left(1 + \binom{23}{1} + \binom{23}{2} + \binom{23}{3} \right) = 2^{23}$$

There is also the perfect ternary code mentioned in §3.7. All these perfect codes were known in 1949. For over twenty years it was conjectured that there are no others. This has recently been established by Van Lint, Tietäväinen, and Perko:

(5.10.4) **Theorem** No unknown perfect codes exist.

§ 5.11 BCH Codes

Bose-Chaudhuri-Hocquenghem (BCH) codes are a large and useful family of codes, with a powerful decoding algorithm.

(5.11.1) **Definition** The **BCH code** of designed distance d $= 2t + 1$ and length n has generator polynomial

$$g(x) = 1.c.m. \{ M^{(1)}(x), M^{(2)}(x), \dots, M^{(2t)}(x) \}$$

This definition is valid for BCH codes over any field GF(q). For binary codes $M^{(2i)}(x) = M^{(i)}(x)$, so

$$g(x) = 1.c.m. \{ M^{(1)}(x), M^{(3)}(x), \dots, M^{(2t-1)}(x) \} \quad .$$

The number of parity checks $= \deg g(x) \leqslant 2mt$ in general, and $\leqslant mt$ for binary codes. The exact determination of the number of parity checks is complicated: see Berlekamp [1], Ch. 12.

(5.11.2) **Theorem** The minimum distance of this code is at least $2t + 1$.

Proof. By Theorem (5.7.1), since $g(x)$ has consecutive roots $\alpha, \alpha^2, \dots, \alpha^{2t}$.

We see from (5.8.1) that Hamming codes are single-error-correcting BCH codes.

The parity check matrix is obtained as follows. A vector $c(x)$ is in the code $\Leftrightarrow c(\alpha) = 0, c(\alpha^2) = 0, \dots, c(\alpha^{2t}) = 0 \Leftrightarrow \Sigma c_i \alpha^i = 0, \Sigma c_i \alpha^{2i} = 0, \dots,$ $\Sigma c_i \alpha^{2it} = 0 \Leftrightarrow Hc^t = 0$, where $c = (c_0, c_1, \dots, c_{n-1})$, and

$$
H \ = \ \begin{bmatrix} 1 & \alpha & \alpha^2 & \cdots & \alpha^{n-1} \\ 1 & \alpha^2 & \alpha^4 & \cdots & \alpha^{2(n-1)} \\ & & \cdots & & \\ 1 & \alpha^{2t} & \alpha^{4t} & \cdots & \alpha^{2t(n-1)} \end{bmatrix} . \tag{5.11.3}
$$

(5.11.4) **Decoding in the Binary Case** Suppose errors occur at locations $i_1,\dots,i_u$; so that $e(x) = \sum_{\nu=1}^{u} x^{i_\nu}$. Define the **error locators** $X_\nu = \alpha^{i_\nu}$, and the **error locator polynomial** $\sigma(z) = \prod_{\nu=1}^{u} (1 - X_\nu z) = \sum_{i=0}^{u} \sigma_i z^i$. By multiplying the received vector by the H matrix the decoder can determine the quantities

$$
S_\ell \ = \ e(\alpha^\ell) \ = \ \sum_{\nu=1}^{u} \alpha^{\ell i_\nu} \ = \ \sum_{\nu=1}^{u} X_\nu^\ell \ , \quad \ell = 1, \dots, 2t.
$$

The decoder's problem is, given $S_1, S_2 \dots, S_{2t}$, to find the most likely error polynomial $e(x)$. It is enough to find $\sigma(z)$, for then the roots of $\sigma(z)$ (which are relatively easy to find) give the error locators.

The coefficients of $\sigma(z)$ are elementary symmetric functions of the X_ν's:

$$
\sigma_0 \ = \ 1 ,
$$

$$
\sigma_1 \ = \ - \sum X_i \ ,
$$

$$
\sigma_2 \ = \ \sum_{i<j} X_i X_j \ ,
$$

$$
\sigma_3 \ = \ - \sum_{i<j<k} X_i X_j X_k \ , \dots ,
$$

whereas the S_ℓ's are the power-sum symmetric functions of the X_ν's.

The relationship between the σ_i and the S_ℓ is given by Newton's identities, which are obtained as follows. Define $\sigma_{u+1} = \sigma_{u+2} = \dots = 0$, so that

$$
\sigma(z) \ = \ \sum_{i=0}^{\infty} \sigma_i z^i \ = \ \prod_{\nu=1}^{u} (1 - X_\nu z) ,
$$

and

$$S(z) = \sum_{\ell=0}^{\infty} S_{\ell} z^{\ell} \ .$$

Then

$$\sigma'(z) = - \sum_{\nu=1}^{u} \frac{X_{\nu} \sigma(z)}{1 - X_{\nu} z} \ ,$$

$$z\sigma'(z) = - \sigma(z) \sum_{\nu=1}^{u} \sum_{r=1}^{\infty} (X_{\nu} z)^{r}$$

$$= - \sigma(z) S(z) \ .$$

I.e.,

(5.11.5) $z\sigma'(z) + \sigma(z) S(z) = 0.$

Equating coefficients we obtain Newton's identities:

$$r\sigma_r + \sum_{i+\ell=r} \sigma_i S_{\ell} = 0$$

or

$$S_1 - \sigma_1 = 0$$

$$S_2 - S_1 \sigma_1 + 2\sigma_2 = 0$$

(5.11.6)

$$S_3 - S_2 \sigma_1 + S_1 \sigma_2 - 3\sigma_3 = 0$$

$$S_4 - S_3 \sigma_1 + S_2 \sigma_2 - S_1 \sigma_3 + 4\sigma_4 = 0$$

It can be shown that, provided $u \leqslant t$, these equations can be solved for the σ_i .

For example, consider a double-error-correcting binary BCH code. The decoder knows S_1 and S_3 (and $S_2 = S_1^2$, $S_4 = S_1^4$). If no errors occur, then $S_1 = S_3 = 0$. If there is a single error in location i, then $S_1 = \alpha^i$, $S_3 = \alpha^{3i} = S_1^3$. If two errors occur, in locations i and j, then $S_1 = \alpha^i + \alpha^j$, $S_3 = \alpha^{3i} + \alpha^{3j}$ and from (5.11.6),

$$S_1 = \sigma_1 \ ,$$

$$S_3 \; - \; S_2 \sigma_1 \; + \; S_1 \sigma_2 \; = \; 0,$$

or

$$\sigma_2 \; = \; \frac{S_3}{S_1} + S_1^2 \; .$$

Thus α^i and α^j are given by the reciprocal roots of the quadratic

$$1 \; + \; S_1 z \; + \; \left(\frac{S_3}{S_1} + S_1^2 \right) z^2 \; .$$

Decoding by solving (5.11.6) is usually the best technique for small values of t. But for larger t an iterative technique due to Berlekamp is to be preferred. It can be stated as an algorithm for finding the shortest feedback shift register that will produce a given output sequence. Several excellent descriptions are available, and we refer the reader to Berlekamp [1] Ch. 7, Massey [102], or Gallager [6] §6.7.

§ 5.12 Reed-Solomon Codes

A Reed-Solomon (RS) code is the special case of a BCH code when $m = 1$, $n = q-1$. Thus an RS code of designed distance d has generator polynomial

$$g(x) \; = \; (x - \alpha) (x - \alpha^2) \ldots (x - \alpha^{d-1}) ,$$

$\alpha \epsilon$ GF(q). The number of check symbols is $r = \deg g(x) = d-1$.

Now the minimum distance of any [n,k] code cannot exceed $n-k+1 = r+1$ (for a codeword with one nonzero information symbol has weight $\leqslant$ $r +1$). Therefore the minimum distance of the RS code is exactly d.

(5.12.1) **Example** The RS code of length $n = 3$ and $d = 2$ over GF(4). We take GF(4) = { $0,1,\alpha,\beta = \alpha^2$ }, with $\alpha^3 = 1$, $\alpha^2 + \alpha + 1 = 0$.

Then $g(x) = x - \alpha$. The 4^2 codewords are

000	$1\alpha 0$	$\beta 0\alpha$	$\beta \alpha 1$
01α	$\alpha\beta 0$	10β	111
$0\alpha\beta$	$\beta 10$	$1\beta\alpha$	$\alpha\alpha\alpha$
$0\beta 1$	$\alpha 01$	$\alpha 1\beta$	$\beta\beta\beta$

Thus Reed-Solomon codes have the parameters

$$[n = q - 1, k, d = n - k + 1] \quad \text{over} \quad GF(q),$$

for all q and all $0 \leqslant k \leqslant q\text{-}1$.

§ 5.13 Justesen Codes

A beautifully simple construction of a sequence of codes which, for any rate R, $0 < R < 1$, have d/n bounded away from zero. Only a sketch of the construction will be given.

The starting point is to take a codeword

$$(a_0, a_1, \dots, a_{N-1})$$

in a Reed-Solomon $[N = 2^m\text{-}1, K, D = N - K + 1]$ code over $GF(2^m)$. Let α be a primitive element of $GF(2^m)$. Form the array

$$(5.13.1) \qquad \begin{pmatrix} a_0 & a_1 & \cdots & a_{N-1} \\ b_0 & b_1 & \cdots & b_{N-1} \end{pmatrix}$$

where $b_i = \alpha^i a_i$, and replace each element in the array by the corresponding binary vector of length m. The resulting $2m \times (2^m\text{-}1)$ binary array is a codeword in the Justesen code, which is therefore a binary linear code of length $n = 2m(2^m\text{-}1)$ and dimension $k = mK$.

E.g., the codeword 01α of (5.12.1) gives the array $\begin{pmatrix} 0 & 1 & \alpha \\ 0 & \alpha & 1 \end{pmatrix}$ and the codeword

$$\begin{pmatrix} 0 & 0 & 1 \\ 0 & 1 & 0 \\ 0 & 1 & 0 \\ 0 & 0 & 1 \end{pmatrix} \quad ,$$

which we could write as 001 010 010 001. Thus (5.12.1) gives a $[12, 4, 4]$ binary Justesen code.

We observe that if $a_i \neq 0$, $a_j \neq 0$, $i \neq j$, then

$$\begin{pmatrix} a_i \\ (\alpha^i) a_i \end{pmatrix} \quad \text{and} \quad \begin{pmatrix} a_j \\ (\alpha^j) a_j \end{pmatrix}$$

produce distinct binary vectors of length 2m. Therefore in each Justesen codeword, there are at least D distinct nonzero binary columns and so each codeword has a large weight.

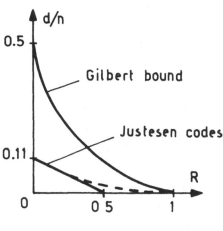

Fig. 5.13.2.

A detailed analysis for which we refer the reader to   35 , now shows that these codes perform at least as well as the heavy line in Fig. 5.13.2.

These codes plainly have rate less than 1/2. To obtain higher rates, the last rows of each binary array are deleted, where s is chosen in the optimal way. The resulting codes behave at least as well as the broken line in Fig. 5.13.2.

§ 5.14 Notes and Further Reading

The material on cyclic codes is standard -see Berlekamp [1] Ch. 5, [3a] Ch. 8, etc. **Encoding**   cyclic codes is very easy using shift registers. We do not have time to describe this here, but instead refer the reader to [1], p. 128, [3a] § 8.7. Cyclic codes are still too large a class to possess a good general decoding algorithm. However, one general method which makes use of the cyclic properties of the code is the **permutation decoding** technique of MacWilliams [101]. The decoding technique given in (3.6.1) for the Golay code, and a similar method described by Tzeng and Zimmerman [113], can also be applied to many cyclic codes of modest length.

§ 5.8 Hamming codes were discovered by Golay [25] and Hamming [30], Elias [95] (see also [1] § 14.84, [3a] p. 134) showed that the direct product of a number of extended Hamming codes gives a sequence of codes whose error probability approaches zero and whose rate is bounded away from zero as the length increases. Nonlinear codes with the same parameters as the Hamming codes were given by Vasil'ev [114]. Nonlinear single-error-correcting which contain more codewords than shortened Hamming codes were given by Sloane and Whitehead [108].

Hamming codes have been used in learning machines [100].

§ 5.9 The method of constructing a Hadamard matrix given here is one of the classical ones, see for example Paley [103]. Many other techniques are known (e.g., Hall [29a] Ch. 14.)

Other nonlinear codes similar to Hadamard codes but based on **conference matrices** have been constructed by Sloane and Seidel [107].

§ 5.9 Simplex codes are also known as **maximum length shift register codes**, or **pseudo noise sequences**, and are of great importance for random number generation, range finding, and other radar applications. (See Golomb [7], [96].)

§ 5.10 For the proof of Theorem (5.10.4) see Van Lint [99], and Tietäväinen [110]-[112].

Unsolved Problem Even though

$$2^{78} \left(1 + \binom{90}{1} + \binom{90}{2}\right) = 2^{90} \quad ,$$

it is known ([2] p. 97) that no perfect [90,78,5] code exists. Is there a [90,77,5] code?

§ 5.11 BCH codes were discovered by Bose, Ray-Chandhuri, and Hocquenghem [91], [98]. See Berlekamp's book [1] for a great deal of additional information related to these codes. Variations on Berlekamp's decoding algorithm, and special decoding techniques for small numbers of errors, have been described by Apple [90], Burton [92], Cowles and Davida [93], Davida [94], Polkinghorn [104], and Sullivan [109].

§ 5.12 Reed-Solomon codes were first described in [105].
§ 5.13 See Justesen [35]. These codes have been used to construct very dense sphere packings in high dimensional Euclidean space [106].

§ 5.15 References

[90] Apple, G.G., Jr. (197), High Speed Double Error Correcting BCH Decoder, to appear.

[91] Bose, R.C. and D.K. Ray-Chaudhuri (1960), On a Class of Error-Correcting Binary Group Codes, IC 3:68-79 and 279-290.

[92] Burton, H.O. (1971A), Inversionless Decoding of Binary BCH Codes, PGIT 17:464-466.

[93] Cowless, J.W. and G.I. Davida (1972), Decoding of Triple-Error-Correcting BCH Codes, Electronics Letters, 8 (Nov: 16).

[94] Davida, G.I. (1971), Decoding of BCH Codes, Electronics Letters 7:664.

[95] Elias, P. (1954), Error-Free Coding, PGIT 4:29-37,

[96] Golomb, S.W. (1967), Shift. Register Sequences, Holden-Day, San Francisco.

[97] Hocquenghem, A. (1959), Codes Correcteurs d'Erreurs, Chiffres 2:147-156.

[98] Van Lint, J.H. (197), A Survey of Perfect Codes, Rocky Mntn. J. Math., to appear.

[99] Lytle, F.E. (1972), Hamming Type Codes Applied to Learning Machine Determinations of Molecular Formulas, Analytical Chemistry 44:1867-1869.

[100] MacWilliams, F.J. (1964) Permutation Decoding of Systematic Codes, BSTJ 43:485-505.

[101] Massey, J. L. (1969), Shift-Register Synthesis and BCH Decoding, PGIT 15:122-127.

[102] Paley, R.E.A.C. (1933), On Orthogonal Matrices, J. Math. Phys. 12:311-320.

[103] Polkinghorn, F., Jr. (1966), Decoding of Double and Triple Error Correcting Bose-Chaudhuri Codes, PGIT 12:480-481.

[104] Reed, I.S. and G. Solomon (1960), Polynomial Codes Over Certain Finite Fields, SIAMJ 8:300-304.

[105] Sloane, N.J.A. (1972a), Dense Sphere Packings Constructed from Error-Correcting Codes, Mathematika 10:183-190.

[106] Sloane, N.J.A. and J.J. Seidel (1970), A New Family of Nonlinear Codes Obtained from Conference Matrices, Annals N.Y. Sciences 175:363-365.

[107] Sloane, N.J.A. and D.S. Whitehead (1970), New Family of Single-Error Correcting Codes, PGIT 16:717-719.

[108] Sullivan, D.D. (1972), A Branching Control Circuit for Berlekamp's BCH Decoding Algorithm, PGIT 18:690-692.

[109] Tietäväinen, A. (1970), On the Nonexistence of Perfect 4-Hamming-Correcting Codes, Ann. Acad.Sci. Fenn., Ser. AI 485:3-6.

[110] Tietäväinen, A. (1973), On the Nonexistence of Perfect Codes Over Finite Fields, SIAMJ 24:88-96.

[111] Tietäväinen, A. and A.Perko (1971), There are No Unknown Perfect Binary Codes, Ann. Univ. Turku., Ser. AI 148:3-10.

[112] Tzeng, K.K. and K. Zimmerman (1972), On Full Power Decoding of Cyclic Codes, Proceeding Princeton Conference on Information Sciences and Systems, 1972, pp. 404-407.

[113] Vasil'ev, J.L. (1962), On Nongroup Close-Packed Codes, Prob. Cybernetics, 8:337-339.

Contents

Page

Printed in the United States
By Bookmasters